IMAGES
of America

AMES

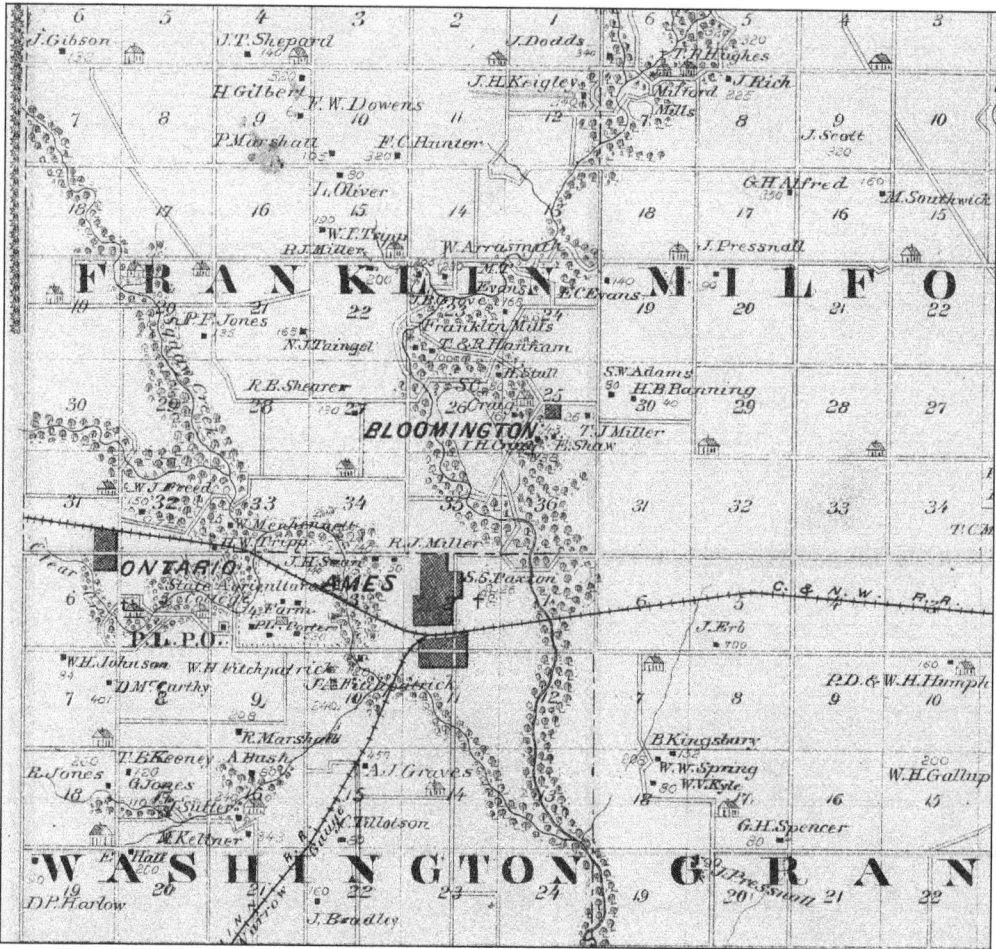

A. T. Andreas' *Illustrated Historical Atlas of the State of Iowa*, 1875, shows the location of Ames, established in 1864 and incorporated in 1870, and Iowa Agricultural College (labeled "Agricultural Farm"), established in 1858, within the context of the surrounding townships of Story County. The towns of Bloomington and Ontario no longer exist; they are now part of the city of Ames. (Courtesy of the Ames Historical Society.)

ON THE COVER: This 1898 photograph depicts the fusion of college and city communities in Ames. A group of Ames citizens and Iowa State College students gather in front of the original Ames depot, built in 1864, to meet the trains bearing visitors to Iowa State for the first Excursion Day. This celebration was designed to introduce to the people of Iowa the work being done at the college. (Courtesy of the Ames Public Library Farwell T. Brown Photographic Archive.)

IMAGES
of America

AMES

Douglas L. Biggs and Gloria J. Betcher

ARCADIA
PUBLISHING

Published by Arcadia Publishing
Charleston, South Carolina

Library of Congress Control Number: 2013949724

For all general information, please contact Arcadia Publishing:
Telephone 843-853-2070
Fax 843-853-0044
E-mail sales@arcadiapublishing.com
For customer service and orders:
Toll-Free 1-888-313-2665

Visit us on the Internet at www.arcadiapublishing.com

To our parents, who nurtured our love of history.

CONTENTS

ACKNOWLEDGMENTS

We would like to thank those who helped us in producing this volume for Arcadia Publishing. While many have provided ideas, located photographs, and offered advice—for which we are grateful—special thanks go to the following people and organizations: The Ames Historical Society and its staff members, especially Dennis Wendell, Casie Vance, Alex Fejfar, and Margaret Vance; the *Ames Tribune* and its editorial and photographic staff; the Special Collections Department of the Iowa State University Library and its staff, especially Becky Jordan; Hank Zalatel and Nelson Electric Company for supplying photographs from their personal collections; the Ames Public Library for allowing us to publish photographs from the Farwell T. Brown Photographic Archive; the Ames Main Street Cultural District; the City of Ames and its staff; and the Iowa Department of Transportation Library and its staff, especially Leighton Christiansen. Thanks also go to the editorial staff at Arcadia, especially Jacel Egan and Maggie Bullwinkel, who have shepherded this book through the publication process.

Images credited as "FTBPA" are part of the Farwell T. Brown Photographic Archive and appear courtesy of the Ames Public Library. Images credited "©*Ames Tribune*. All rights reserved" are *Ames Tribune* photographs, provided courtesy of the Ames Historical Society and the *Ames Tribune*. Images credited "AHS" are part of the Ames Historical Photographic Archive and appear courtesy of the Ames Historical Society. Images credited "Photograph copyright ©IADOT. All rights reserved" appear courtesy of the Iowa Department of Transportation. Images credited "Special Collections, ISU Library" appear courtesy of the Special Collections Department of the Iowa State University Library.

INTRODUCTION

The bustling, 21st-century city today called Ames began as two separate communities: Iowa Agricultural College (now Iowa State University), founded in 1858, and Ames Station, founded in 1864 as a stopping point for water and coal on John Insley Blair's railway line. Until Blair bought land for his depot from Cynthia Duff, what would become Ames was nothing more than an unincorporated collection of farmsteads in the sparsely populated western portion of Story County. The college founders, who initially sought to keep their students away from the vices of city living, looked on as Ames developed. In time, the communities became keenly aware of their mutual dependence, but the two miles of Squaw Creek bottomland between them was a major barrier to both communication and transportation in the 19th century. In periods of flood or heavy snow, the college was isolated from the town—and vice versa—for days or even a week at a time. As separate communities, Ames never reached more than 1,276 residents, and Iowa Agricultural College never grew beyond 336 students.

The relationship changed because of the vision of local Ames businessman Judge John L. Stevens, who in 1891 gathered a group of local investors and cobbled together enough money to build a two-mile steam rail line they called the Ames & College Railway (or "the Dinkey"). Suddenly, the trip between town and college that had often taken hours now took only eight minutes in all kinds of weather. Students and faculty began to live in town, and townspeople began to take the Dinkey to the college for evening events and public lectures. In 1893, Ames annexed the land around the college, and the two communities rapidly became one. The city saw a boom in business, and its population grew by 89.8 percent from 1890 to 1900, reaching more than 4,200 people—the greatest period of growth in Ames's history.

Forging one community bore fruit, and as Ames became more prominent in state and national affairs, it also grew as a transportation hub. Visits by presidents, such as Theodore Roosevelt, William Howard Taft, Dwight Eisenhower, and Barack Obama; political candidates, like Ronald Reagan, Bill Bradley, Michelle Bachman, and Hillary Clinton; civil rights leaders, such as Rev. Jesse Jackson and Rev. Dr. Martin Luther King Jr.; and world leaders, like Nikita Khrushchev, have confirmed Ames and Iowa State University as places of significance to the global community. Ames has also been geographically significant to the state and region. Centrally located in Iowa, the city is a natural spot for transportation and communication lines to merge. By 1874, Ames sat at the crossroads of major north-south and east-west railroads. Although passenger rail service to Ames ceased in 1960, the Union Pacific Railroad still runs over 50 freight trains a day through town. In 1913, Ames gained a spot on the Lincoln Highway/ US Highway 30; in 1924, the Iowa Highway Commission built its headquarters in town; and in 1929, US Highway 69 came through the city. By the time the Federal Highway Commission placed Interstate 35 near Ames in the 1960s, the community had established itself as a regional center for commerce, technology, and education.

Throughout the 20th century, research and development conducted in Ames changed the lives of people in Iowa and around the world. In the early decades of the 20th century, Dr. W.B.

Niles, along with Drs. M. Dorset and C.N. McBryde, worked in Ames to develop a vaccine for hog cholera, which led to the eradication of this terrible disease in the United States. During World War II, a team of Iowa State College scientists led by Profs. Frank Spedding and Harley Wilhelm developed the process for refining the first weapons-grade uranium for the Manhattan Project, and in 1939, Ames saw the development of the world's first digital computer by John Atanasoff and his student Clifford Berry.

Since 1920, when Ames adopted the city manager form of government, eight men have sure-handedly managed the affairs of the city. Two, John H. Ames and Steven L. Schainker, served for a combined 57 of these 93 years. Under both men, Ames has seen improvements in public utilities, with new and/or expanded electric, water, wastewater treatment, and solid-waste disposal facilities, as well as improvements to the police and fire departments, among other things. Such consistent leadership and careful stewardship of the city's financial resources have helped enable Ames to effectively weather the storms of depressions, recessions, and downturns in the agricultural economy, as well as the storms of nature. Repeated floods have inundated the city throughout its history, destroying infrastructure but not the will of the community to rebuild and renew. Fires have burned significant portions of the Downtown and the university, but new buildings have filled the gaps with little difficulty. Resilience has enabled the town founded on swampy ground as a railway water station to survive and thrive, first as a small community, and then as a modern city.

By 2010, the city's population had reached nearly 60,000. Ames moved into the 21st century with a regional airport; light manufacturing industries, such as Danfoss, Hach Chemical, Barilla, and 3M; and a wealth of big box stores, like Target, K-Mart, Best Buy, Lowes, and Wal-Mart, common to most towns its size. Yet in spite of development, growth, and change, for 150 years, Ames has remained true to its roots as a railroad town and a university community. The people of the city continue to join philanthropic and social organizations, such as the Ames Woman's Club, Rotary International, Kiwanis, the Masonic Temple, and the Elks, that serve their fellow citizens. Community spirit still manifests itself in the generous work of volunteers for the Ames Public Library, Ames Animal Shelter, Food at First, Youth & Shelter Services, and the Volunteer Center of Story County; the public lectures sponsored by organizations like the Ames Historical Society and University Lectures Committee; parades, such as those held to celebrate VEISHEA, Memorial Day, and the Fourth of July; and the artistic and cultural events sponsored by the likes of Ames Community Arts Council, Ames Town & Gown, ACTORS, the Main Street Cultural District, the Campustown Action Association, and the Octagon Center for the Arts. All of these aspects of community contribute to the high quality of life in this university town, which repeatedly has been recognized by national publications. Ames receives high marks for an intelligent workforce, excellent water quality, walkable neighborhoods, retirement amenities, and an affordable university education, to name just a few of the recent accolades.

The legacy of Ames's founders—fortitude, ingenuity, and progressivism—continues to inform and inspire successive generations of Ames citizens. When Cynthia Duff bought land from Lucian Hoggatt and, in turn, sold it to John Insley Blair to build his depot, she had no idea that her savvy business decision would have such far-reaching and successful consequences.

One

SOLID FOUNDATIONS, 1864–1893

When Story County, Iowa, was first settled in the 1850s, no one gave any thought to placing a town in the swampy bottomland near the confluence of the Skunk River and Squaw Creek. Most of the county's population lay east of the Skunk, a major barrier to travel westward. The establishment of the state's agricultural college and model farm in 1858 on the isolated prairie west of the Squaw gave even the institution's founders pause to consider whether they had chosen the right location. They need not have worried. John Insley Blair brought his Chicago & North Western Railroad through the central part of the state in 1864, opening the way for more settlement in the area. All of this development came at a price, though. Local farmers, realizing the great wealth of the railroad, would sell land to Blair only at inflated prices. To avoid these exorbitant charges, Blair chose to purchase bottomland in Washington Township that was considered unworthy for any other purpose and build his station there. That station stop, built on land purchased from Cynthia Duff and named Ames Station after Blair's friend US congressman Oakes Ames, became the town of Ames. Settlers in the township soon saw a thriving town spring up around Blair's railway station stop. For the first 27 years of Ames's existence (1864–1891), the town and the college two miles to its west across the Squaw Creek developed as independent communities. The two were intimately aware of each other but remained essentially independent until local visionaries found the means—political, social, and physical—to bind them together. Then, in 1891, the Ames & College Railway united the two communities. These early years set a solid foundation for building the strong community that became the city of Ames.

The model farm began operations in 1858. One of the earliest images of farm activities from about 1875 shows students working with horses. The Civil War delayed construction of a main college building until 1864. Poor workmanship led to the demolition of that original building before it was occupied. (Special Collections, ISU Library.)

Shown here in 1885, the College Building (later known as "the Main"), housing classrooms, dormitories, and offices, finally opened in 1868. The first class of students arrived for a preparatory term that autumn, and classes began on campus in January 1869. Splendid as the Main appeared, however, it had inadequate indoor sanitation and soon became cramped quarters for the growing college. (Special Collections, ISU Library.)

When the first 173 students arrived at the Iowa State Agricultural College, the nation's first coeducational land grant college, they found a campus under the leadership of Adonijah S. Welch, the college's first president, who served from 1869 to 1883. Welch had experience at the helm of new colleges, having been the first principal of Michigan State Normal School (Eastern Michigan University) from 1851 to 1865. In his role as president at Iowa State, Welch was instrumental in developing the agriculture and mechanical arts curriculum, and he supported the right of women to receive college degrees at the school alongside men. He is also credited with planting the first trees on campus, beautifully defining the school's grounds within the surrounding prairie. Although Welch resigned the college presidency in 1883 because of pressure from colleagues who did not share his vision for the institution's advancement, he continued to teach at the school as the chair of History of Civilization and Practical Psychology until his death in 1889. (Special Collections, ISU Library.)

11

Shortly after Iowa State Agricultural College was established in Washington Township, pioneer settlers Lucian and Abigail Hoggatt donated an acre of land for a school, later named Hoggatt School. Built between 1861 and 1862 north of Boone Street, near the intersection with Maple Avenue, the one-room school predated the railroad's arrival in Ames. The building was later incorporated into a home and restored in 1981, as shown in this photograph. (FTBPA.)

Cynthia Olive Kellogg Duff, shown here around 1870, and her husband, Alexander, purchased land in Washington Township in 1863. One portion of that land was sold to John Insley Blair in 1864 for the construction of the Chicago & North Western Railroad's Ames Station. A second portion was platted as the town of Ames in December 1864. City assessor's records now identify those parcels as the "Original Town." (FTBPA.)

John Insley Blair's Chicago & North Western Railroad constructed the first building in Ames— the railway depot—in 1864 on land purchased from Cynthia and Alexander Duff. In this 1867 photograph of the depot, an array of railroad workers line the south side of the tracks at the east end of what became the business district (now called "Downtown"). (FTBPA.)

By 1870, Ames had elected its first mayor, William West (1822–1920), the proprietor of the West Hotel on Douglass (now Douglas) Avenue. Mayor West, a former Ohio legislator, served only three months of his one-year term before passing the office to interim mayor W.D. Lucas (1838–1892), a local banker, in 1871. Lucas served a second mayoral term from 1874 to 1875. (FTBPA.)

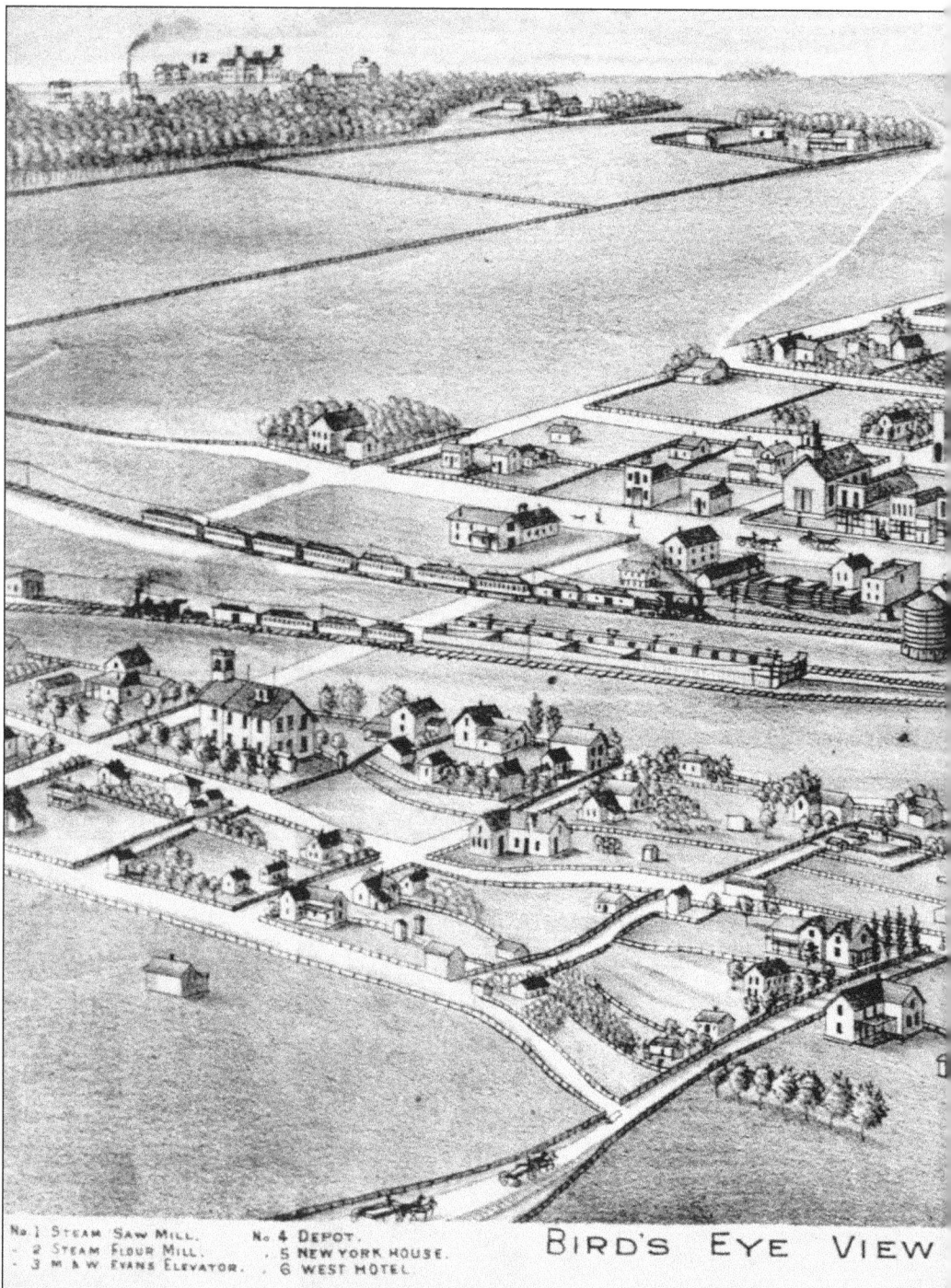

BIRD'S EYE VIEW

This 1875 "Bird's Eye View of Ames, Story Co., Iowa" shows the depot (No. 4) just south of the M&W Evans Elevator (No. 3). Other key buildings include the following businesses and public institutions: Steam Saw Mill (No. 1), Steam Flour Mill (No. 2), New York House (No. 5), West Hotel (No. 6); Methodist Episcopal church (No. 7), Baptist church (No. 8), Congregational church (No. 9), North Public School (No. 10), South Public School (No. 11), and Iowa State

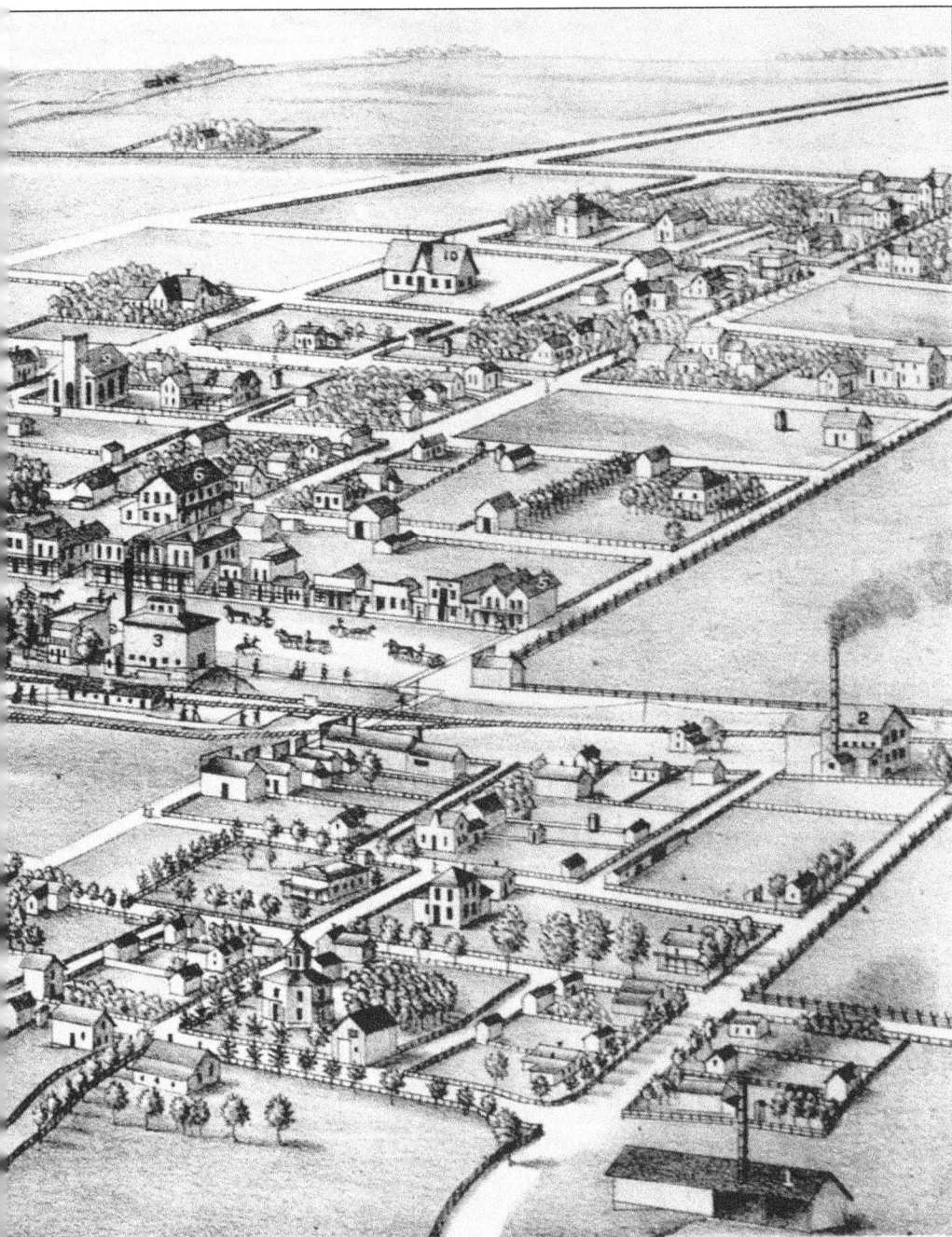

Agricultural College (No. 12). The depiction shows an idyllic town with tree-lined neighborhoods and smooth streets thronged with wagons. What settlers actually contended with was a marshy area of interconnected sloughs that left little room between the Skunk River and the Squaw Creek to build tidy homes on smooth, dry streets and more often mired wagons up to their hubs in mud. (FTBPA.)

A typical Ames residence of 1866 was more farmhouse than city dwelling. This house built by Vanderlyn "Van" Chamberlain, who came to Ames in 1865 and later became manager of Queal, Hostler & Boards lumberyard, is reputedly similar to the first house in Ames built by Noah Webster in 1864 at the corner of Douglass (now Douglas) Avenue and Story (now Fifth) Street. (FTBPA.)

Prosperous residents, like successful merchant Daniel Bigelow (left), could afford homes that suited their status. Bigelow arrived in Ames in 1866 and opened a dry goods store with partner Henry Huntington in 1867. In the late 1860s, around the time George Galen Tilden joined the firm to create the longtime partnership of Bigelow, Huntington & Tilden, Bigelow built the house on Duff Avenue pictured in this 1870s photograph. (FTBPA.)

Aware of national trends even in 1875, Ames celebrated Memorial Day with a parade of veterans only two years after the holiday was first officially recognized in New York in 1873. More than 130 Civil War veterans lie buried in the Ames Municipal Cemetery, among them many prominent Ames residents, such as Daniel Bigelow, Kendrick Brown, George G. and Frederick Tilden, Iraneous Smith, and Wallace Greeley. (FTBPA.)

Onondaga Street (renamed Main Street in 1910) still comprised mostly wood-framed buildings in the 1880s. Like many businesses shown in this photograph of the north side of the street, the New York Store (at left), owned by a New York native named I.E. Hirsh, had opened in the 1860s or 1870s. (FTBPA.)

Eight years after the town's first school was constructed, Ames voters approved the formation of a school district in 1870 for Subdistrict 4 of Washington Township. By that time, Ames classes had long since left Hoggatt School and had moved to a two-story building south of Boone Street (now Lincoln Way). The district served 141 students in its first year, with two teachers and a budget of $1,792.33. In 1872, the new district had already enrolled enough students that extra space had to be rented in town. By 1874, two lots had been purchased for a new schoolhouse, and the following year, a $2,000 bond issue paid for a new four-room school on the corner of Eighth Street and Kellogg Avenue. Only 11 years after its founding, what came to be called the Ames School District had constructed its first brick school on the west side of Clark Avenue between Story (now Fifth) Street and Sixth Street. This building housed the only school serving the community during the 1880s and 1890s. (FTBPA.)

Fires in 1886 and 1887 destroyed many of the wood-framed business buildings on the north side of Onondaga (Main) Street between Douglass (Douglas) Avenue and Kellogg Avenue. Wooden sidewalks, like the one on which the band stands in this 1885 photograph, contributed to the fires. In the 1880s, Ames had no fire department and no waterworks. As one resident remembered, all anyone could do was watch the buildings burn. (FTBPA.)

As Ames grew, Iowa State Agricultural College, two miles west, also thrived, independent of the town's influence. In 1888, the college still stood in almost complete isolation on the high prairie. Beyond the cluster of college buildings on the west edge of campus, captured by a photographer from the top of the Main, fields and trees stretch to the horizon. (Special Collections, ISU Library.)

For many years, the Main was the college. Students, faculty, and staff lived, ate, and attended lectures and labs all in one building. Overcrowding became a problem as enrollment increased. Sanitary conditions posed a constant concern, and in the 1870s, three-story "sanitary towers" for bathroom facilities were added at the end of each wing (they are the short structures on the wings in the foreground). (Special Collections, ISU Library.)

The poor condition of Boone Street (now Lincoln Way), the primary road across Squaw Creek, contributed to the college's continued isolation. Muddy conditions, like those in this 1909 photograph, often hampered travel on the horse-drawn omnibus, the only transportation between town and college until a rail link was established in 1891. Reports of mud up to vehicles' wheel hubs were common until the road was paved in the 1920s. (FTBPA.)

President Chamberlain's departure in November 1890 led the Iowa Agricultural College's board of trustees to offer the presidency to William Miller Beardshear, superintendent of Des Moines Public Schools, seen in this official portrait taken in 1891. Beardshear took office in January 1891. Within months, he began building strong links between the college and the town; the Ames & College Railway was one outgrowth of these efforts. During his 11-year presidency, the college grew from 425 students to over 1,000. As Beardshear developed the agricultural offerings at the college, he added leading faculty in civil engineering, agricultural extension, physics, electrical engineering, agricultural chemistry, and mathematics, among other disciplines. He also lobbied the board of trustees to acquire funds for the construction of new campus buildings—Morrill Hall, 1891; Old Botany (now Catt Hall), 1892; Margaret Hall, 1895; and the Campanile, 1899— all but one of which are still in use today. Before his untimely death following a heart attack in 1902, he had secured his place as one of the most influential presidents of Iowa State. (Special Collections, ISU Library.)

The primary mover behind the Ames & College Railway was Judge John L. Stevens (left), a member of Iowa Agricultural College's first graduating class (1872). A self-styled progressive, he worked to bring material and economic improvements to Ames. In the 1870s, he helped Ames acquire telephone service, and in 1890, he provided the willpower to make a rail link between Ames and the college a reality. (Special Collections, ISU Library.)

The Motor Line, or the Dinkey, was the catalyst for Ames and the Iowa Agricultural College to become one community. This 1900 photograph shows all the assets of the Ames & College Railway: both engines and the entire complement of rolling stock. The flatcar appears at left in the picture, followed by the "immigrant" car and the two passenger cars. (FTBPA.)

One of the most recognizable citizens of Ames in the 1890s was Henry P. "Hank" Wilkinson, the redoubtable conductor of the Motor Line. He worked on the Ames & College Railway from 1892 to 1907 and saw to the safety of passengers during these years. In this picture from the 1905 yearbook, the *Iowa State College Bomb*, Hank stands on the platform of one of the railcars. (Special Collections, ISU Library.)

Another addition to Iowa State College was the Hub, also called "the Dinkey Station," built in 1892 as a waiting room for Ames & College Railway passengers. The building also served as the college bookstore and post office. This photograph, taken before 1907 (when the rail line was electrified), shows the Hub in its original location south of the Central Building (Beardshear). (Photograph copyright ©IADOT. All rights reserved.)

In 1891, construction on Kellogg Avenue included both a water tower, to minimize the threat of another devastating fire Downtown, and the Opera House Block, built by Judge John L. Stevens and professor of horticulture Joseph L. Budd. Seen here in 1897, that building had two commercial stores on the first floor, while the second story, the opera house, provided the largest open floor in Ames, seating 600. (FTBPA).

Mayor Parley Sheldon (1844–1932) supported the creation of the railway linking the town and the campus. This link enabled the annexation of Iowa Agricultural College into the city in 1892–1893, which made the town a City of the Second Class (population 2,000). Sheldon moved to Ames in 1875, became mayor for the first time in 1884, and served in that office eight times over the next 32 years. (FTBPA.)

Two

BUSINESS AND BOOSTERISM

From its origins on Onondaga (Main) Street to its expansion westward to Campustown and southward down Duff Avenue, Ames's business community has supported the success and stability of the city's economy over the decades. Business owners and community boosters, like early members of the Ames Commercial Club (a forerunner of the Ames Chamber of Commerce) Parley Sheldon, Wallace Greeley, and the Munn family, helped to develop Ames as a thriving commercial nexus for central Iowa. A spirit of community boosterism promoted the city's progress in many other ways and is evident throughout Ames's history. The message comes through in the businesses that established themselves as mainstays of Main Street and Boone Street/Lincoln Way, as well as in the city's iconic buildings, like the 1908 Champlin Building and the 1916 Sheldon-Munn Hotel. Strong financial institutions, like the Union National Bank, Story County Bank & Trust, and First National Bank, funded businesses and home purchases even in the lean years of the Great Depression, and Ames's benevolent organizations and philanthropic private citizens, like grocer Abe Mezvinsky, laid the foundation for the strong community of today.

Mud on Onondaga (Main) Street continued to plague travelers into the 20th century, as this 1907 photograph illustrates. Some things had changed, however. Following the fires of the 1880s, the buildings of the business district are mostly brick, and the sidewalks paved. Power lines stretch westward from the municipal electric plant, established in 1896, at the east end of the street, where the Dinkey waits near its shed. (FTBPA.)

From its origins as a wood-framed, fire-prone commercial district in the 1800s, Ames's Downtown, by the time of this 1915 photograph, had emerged as a modern Main Street, complete with wooden creosote pavers, brick commercial buildings, electric streetcar service and lighting, and an ornate Odd Fellows temple (the tallest building at left). (FTBPA.)

In 1908, as electricity became available in Ames homes, Charles "Ben" Nelson recognized the growing need for electrical technicians. He founded Nelson Electric, a family-run company that still serves the Ames community 105 years later. In this 1914 photograph, Agatha "Aggie" Nelson, Ben's wife, stands behind the counter, prepared to sell fixtures, lightbulbs, lamps, and electrical appliances for the modern home. (Photograph courtesy of Nelson Electric.)

When businessman Albert L. Champlin constructed a brick store on his property at the southeast corner of what was then Boone Street and Welch Avenue in 1908, he not only brought a sense of permanence to his longtime commercial endeavors at this location; he planted the seeds of Ames's second business district, known colloquially as "Dogtown" in this early period. (AHS photograph, courtesy of the Champlin family.)

The entrepreneurial efforts of business owners and the growth of Iowa State College encouraged expansion of the Dogtown business district in Ames's fourth ward. By 1916, the year after this photograph was taken, perceived inequities in allocation of city funds had led to the attempted (unsuccessful) secession of "West Ames" from the city. A 1922 contest sponsored by fourth ward merchants gave the business district its current name: Campustown. (FTBPA.)

The Sheldon-Munn Hotel opened Downtown in 1916 and served for many years as luxury hotel, retail building, and conference center for Ames. Success of the hotel project required the initiative of local businessmen Parley Sheldon, president of the Story County Bank, and Hiram L. and Alfred H. Munn, of the Munn Lumber Company; the financial support of the citizens of Ames; and the social commitment of community organizations and Iowa State College. (AHS).

Ames flew flags on Main Street to celebrate the Fourth of July in 1919, but many Ames citizens went to nearby Nevada, Iowa, for the big Victory Day welcome-home for soldiers and sailors of Story County returning from World War I. The Odd Fellows Hall had been rebuilt after burning in 1917, and Carr Hardware, Judisch Brothers, and Tilden's Store were already well established. (AHS photograph, courtesy of Helen Zook.)

This 1920 photograph of the Tilden grocery store at 409–413 Douglas Avenue provides an inside look at a business owned by one of Ames's longest-operating commercial dynasties. The Tilden family had been in the dry goods and grocery business since George G. Tilden joined Bigelow and Huntington in the late 1860s. From left to right are George Miller, Elizabeth (Batman) Salyers, Lucian C. Tilden, and Jim Likely. (FTBPA.)

Ames citizens and businesses contributed generously to the 1931 Red Cross aid campaign for drought sufferers in southern states. Over 1,000 people donated food to gain admission to the Capitol Theater for two benefit movies sponsored by the *Ames Times-Tribune* and the Ames Theatre Company, founded by Joe V. Gerbracht (front left) in 1912. Gerbracht owned four theaters in Ames when he retired in 1962. (AHS.)

Construction on the Grand Avenue/US Highway 69 underpass started in 1937, and local businesses—like Ben Cole & Son, whose truck appears here—worked on the project. The Coles, Ames contractors since at least 1870, when Ben's father, John, contracted for Central High School, also built the Masonic Temple (1916), the Cranford Apartments (1922), and the "new" high school (1938), among other structures. (Photograph copyright ©IADOT. All rights reserved.)

Businesswomen were and are an integral part of the Ames business community. In this October 1948 photograph, Mayor William L. Allen signs a proclamation of Business Women's Week in Ames. The national event, celebrated since 1928, has since 1938 fallen during the third full week in October. (©*Ames Tribune*. All rights reserved.)

Emerhoff Peterson's shoe store, opened on Main Street in 1940, remains one of Ames's most resilient businesses. The store's 1949 remodeling, shown here, added a neon sign. In 1956, the store expanded into 215 and 219 Main Street and added a men's department. Today, the Peterson family store still thrives, and the facade has been updated (2012) to stay in step with times. (©*Ames Tribune*. All rights reserved.)

During World War II, the workers in Collegiate Manufacturing Company's Lechner Building sewing room, pictured in this 1944 photograph, produced not only the company's usual selection of college souvenirs but also rain coats and ponchos for the war effort. Collegiate Manufacturing began operation in 1904 as Tilden's Manufacturing Company. Over the decades of its existence, the company produced many popular items for the national market, including stuffed animals in school colors, mascots, college pennants, felt hats, and other fan gear. They also designed especially for "grown-ups" and "young sociables and their 'BYOL' [Bring Your Own Liquor] parties," Bottle Babies—plush toys that could conceal a bottle of booze. Collegiate closed up shop in Ames in the 1980s. (FTBPA.)

By 1949, many of the businesses found on the north side of Main Street in 1919 had moved to other locations, but Judisch Brothers and Tilden's remain. The American Legion Hall (the Odd Fellows Building) and the old Opera House Block on the corner of Kellogg Avenue and Main Street provide familiar landmarks amid the plain facades stripped of their Victorian trim. (©*Ames Tribune*. All rights reserved.)

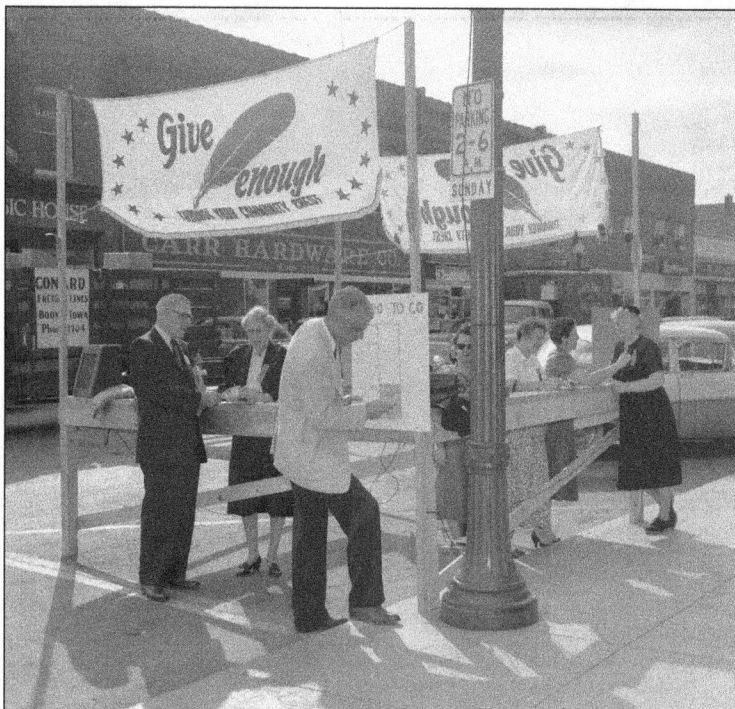

Community spirit shines through in this 1956 photograph of the Ames Community Chest Fund Drive on Main Street. The Ames Community Chest, the common name for the Ames United Fund, founded in 1953, became the United Way of Story County in 1985. Carr Hardware appears in the background of this picture. The store had moved from the north side of Main Street in the 1920s. (©*Ames Tribune*. All rights reserved.)

Kindergarten students enjoyed a field trip to the Ames HyVee grocery store in 1956. The store employed 53 people in 1960 and had expanded by then to add bakery and fresh meat sections. By 2013, HyVee had two Ames locations, featuring amenities like a deli section, in-store banking, dining services, a dry cleaner, a pharmacy, and a well-stocked wine-and-spirits shop. (©*Ames Tribune*. All rights reserved.)

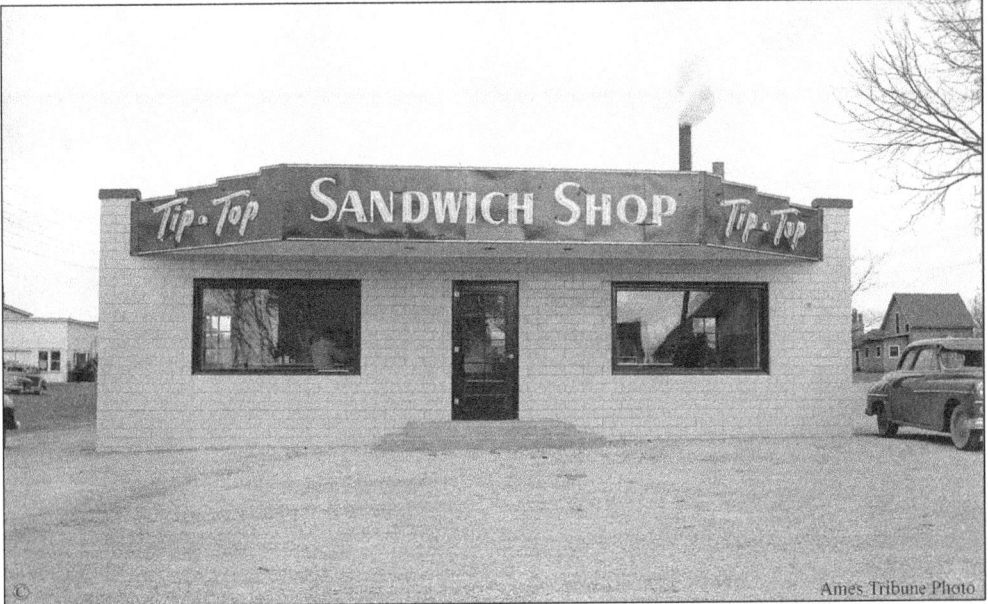

When Robert "Bob" Jones and his wife opened the Tip-Top Sandwich Shop in December 1950, they started an Ames tradition. The business has changed over the decades, but the Tip-Top Lounge still occupies the building on East Lincoln Way and attracts game-day tailgaters looking for a bowl of signature chili and a beer before watching the Iowa State Cyclones hit the gridiron. (©*Ames Tribune*. All rights reserved.)

The Ames Centennial Parade in 1964 offered an opportunity for businesses and boosters in the Ames community to celebrate the area's rich history. Here, the Ames Community Chest float features the young people of the community—Boy and Girl Scouts and members of the YMCA—standing in front of bonneted Granny in her chair, representing the older generation and days gone by. (FTBPA.)

Fast-food restaurants and filling stations met the needs of Lincoln Highway travelers in this 1966 photograph, taken a few blocks west of Duff Avenue, looking east. Before the construction of the bypass for US Highway 30 (the "Main Street of America") to the south of Ames in 1967 and 1968, the thoroughfare showed the hallmarks of highway-oriented commercial development for the automobile age. (©*Ames Tribune*. All rights reserved.)

Penney's and Bledsoe's anchor the corner of Burnett Avenue and Main Street in this 1968 photograph. Bledsoe's had remodeled the old two-story C.G. Lee Building into a one-story, modern design in 1964, and in 1967, the city's purchase of the railroad property south of Main Street had facilitated the creation of a pedestrian mall, now Tom Evans Park, where the 300 block of Burnett used to run. (FTBPA.)

This 1971 photograph encapsulates much of Ames's banking history. On the corner of Burnett Avenue and Fifth Street stands the new building of the First National Bank, founded as Ames Savings Bank in 1903. Across Fifth Street, a sign marks the Union Story Trust & Savings Bank, created in 1932 from the merger of two older banks: the Union National Bank and the Story County Trust & Savings Bank. (FTBPA.)

Grocer Abe Mezvinsky—pictured here in 1978, when he retired—was known throughout Ames, the state, and the Jewish community for his philanthropy. He owned three Ames Fruit & Grocery Company stores between the 1930s and 1970s. Mezvinsky was famously generous, helping out neighbors, employees, and hobos, cosigning loans, assisting people in buying cars and houses, and even facilitating the building of those houses. (©*Ames Tribune*. All rights reserved.)

With the expansion of the Downtown business section to South Duff Avenue in the 1960s came a new challenge for business owners—flooding. In 1993, and several times since, floodwaters covered Duff Avenue, breaking water mains, flooding buildings, and forcing some long-time businesses to close, unable to keep their heads above water as neighboring new construction rose on berms above the 100-year flood level. (©*Ames Tribune*. All rights reserved.)

Three

ROADS, RAILWAYS, AND FORWARD PROGRESS

Ames, it seems, has always sat at a crossroads. For its first half century, the city stood at the crossing of the Chicago & North Western Railway's north-south and east-west lines through Iowa. After the development of the Lincoln Highway in the 1910s and 1920s, Ames lay on the original "Main Street of America," the highway designated Iowa's official east-west interstate route in 1945. Even after the new US Highway 30 bypass opened south of Ames in 1968, the city was still within easy range of this important artery and soon grew alongside it. With the completion of Interstate 35 between Des Moines and the Minnesota border in 1965, Ames, just to its west, had access to a major north-south interstate highway through the mid-section of the country. This access came none too soon, as the Chicago & North Western Railway, Ames's longest-standing rapid transit connection to the region, ceased its passenger service to Ames in 1960. From roads and railways, Ames moved on to add bus systems, taxis, and airports to its transportation network, all under the purview of the Iowa Department of Transportation (formerly the Iowa Highway Commission), which got its start in Ames and continues to be a major influence and employer in the community. This breadth of connectivity and the state college, now university, located in the city have made and continue to make Ames a bustling center of forward progress.

Railroads have always formed Ames's backbone; the city would not exist without them. The largest railway running through Ames was the Chicago & North Western Railroad. Here, in about 1917, two passenger trains pass, one leaving and the other arriving at the Ames depot. This facility was designed by Charles Sumner Frost and built to replace the old depot at the east end of Onondaga (Main) Street in 1900. (FTBPA.)

In 1906, the Ames & College Railway sold out to the larger Fort Dodge, Des Moines & Southern Railway, which electrified and expanded rapid transit service throughout west Ames. The electric streetcars, pictured here gliding down Onondaga (Main) Street in about 1910, were blamed for damaging the facades of the left four buildings in this photograph; the fronts of all four had to be replaced in 1917. (FTBPA.)

This interurban car, pictured at the Fort Dodge, Des Moines & Southern Railway station in Ames that was built in 1914, was one of many that ran on the line linking Ames to cities throughout central Iowa. The railway earned a significant amount of money on freight and the sale of electricity to small towns and farms before selling out to the Chicago & North Western in 1968. (Courtesy of Hank Zalatel.)

In the 1910s, Boone Street mud still plagued unlucky vehicles. By 1913, however, automobile enthusiasts and entrepreneurs at the national level had called for the creation of a highway as a direct route between New York and San Francisco. Boone Street became part of this Lincoln Highway shortly thereafter. The Lincoln Highway was paved by the 1930s, leaving behind the quagmire of the past. (Photograph copyright ©IADOT. All rights reserved.)

The new Lincoln Highway had its challenges, however. Heavy spring and early-summer rains in 1918 led to serious flooding that caused the failure of six bridges around Ames, including the 1908 bridge across Squaw Creek on Lincoln Way. Here, four men (left center) examine the wrecked automobile (far left) of the E.E. Goddard family, who were caught in the collapse but survived. (Photograph copyright ©IADOT. All rights reserved.)

Even in the 1920s, after Boone Street had become part of the Lincoln Highway, the road was still a dirt track. Here, a workman grades the major thoroughfare with a team of horses. Paving of Lincoln Way between Riverside Avenue and Beech (now Beach) Avenue occurred in 1921, but sections farther west took longer to complete. (Photograph copyright ©IADOT. All rights reserved.)

42

The Iowa State Highway Commission, whose facilities are pictured here sometime after 1930, was founded in 1904 as part of Iowa State College of Agriculture & Mechanic Arts. The commission moved into its new headquarters building on Lincoln Way in 1924. Today, this facility forms the core of a larger, more modern structure on the campus of the Iowa Department of Transportation. (Photograph copyright ©IADOT. All rights reserved.)

Omnibuses, like the one in this picture from the 1920s, quickly replaced the streetcar as the city's chosen mode of rapid transit. Bus competition for the Fort Dodge, Des Moines & Southern Railway inspired that railway itself to enter the bus-lines business in 1929 and cease operation that year as a streetcar service in Ames. (Courtesy of Hank Zalatel.)

Pavement-materials testers, such as this team at the Iowa Highway Commission shown with test-pavement sections, helped to ensure that the roadbeds of Iowa's newly paved highways were of the best quality and could stand up to rigorous conditions. (Photograph copyright ©IADOT. All rights reserved.)

By the late 1920s, service stations began to appear on the Lincoln Highway. This one, on the northeast corner of Lincoln Way and Hyland Avenue, was owned by Minos Fall (center) and offered peanuts, popcorn, and candy in addition to gasoline, much like modern convenience stores in the early 21st century. An automobile service garage still stands on this site in 2013. (FTBPA.)

Red Top Cab Company and other taxi services made it possible for Ames citizens and college students, like the two young ladies shown in this 1924 photograph, to catch a train at the Ames depot with the aid of an automobile. The two modes of transportation complemented each other in the modern world of 1920s transport. (Courtesy of Hank Zalatel.)

Heavy rail traffic on the Chicago & North Western main line, combined with increased street traffic heading north and south on Grand Avenue/US Highway 69, led to the construction of an underpass in 1937 and 1938 that took Grand Avenue under two railroad lines and the western end of Main Street. (Photograph copyright ©IADOT. All rights reserved.)

By 1924 Ames had an airport, built by the Gerbracht brothers, Wilford and Joe, for the Gerbracht Aeronautic Corporation. The 40-acre site had three runways used by local pilots, and Wilford gave flying lessons in the company plane, the *Pegasus*. By 1938, Ames had two small airports, and the aeronautical club wanted the city to build a municipal airport so the city could be a stop for the US Post Office Department. The year 1940 brought the establishment of Howard Flying Service's larger airfield on East Thirteenth Street to serve the federal government's Civilian Flight Training Program, which became the War Training Service Program when the United States entered World War II. Ames's municipal airport would finally come in 1944, when the war was well underway, with the completion of four hangars and two runways. (Both, FTBPA.)

The Union Bus Depot in the 400 block of Main Street, completed in February 1949, housed the Overland Café, where weary travelers could rest and enjoy a cup of coffee as they awaited the next of some 25 intercity buses to stop at the depot each day. (Courtesy of Hank Zalatel.)

In 1960, Lincoln Way was a busy US highway. Heavy car and truck traffic through Campustown led to the widening of Lincoln Way to four lanes in 1963 and 1964. Crossing the street could be dangerous, and by 1968, the Ames City Council was considering pedestrian bridges across the road. These bridges were never constructed, perhaps because the completion of the new US 30 bypass reduced traffic. (Photograph copyright ©IADOT. All rights reserved.)

The automobile had firmly supplanted rail as the preferred mode of long-distance travel in Iowa by the time of this 1969 photograph. Lincoln Way, looking east from the Highway Commission, shows no evidence of the dirt track of 1913, and a four-lane highway and King's restaurant stand where the Fort Dodge, Des Moines & Southern depot once did. (Photograph copyright ©IADOT. All rights reserved.)

By the 1970s, Ames needed a new and expanded bus service. The city and university developed a partnership in this public-transportation endeavor and called the new service CyRide. The campus was now linked to all parts of the city via this bus service, and university students could affordably live in any part of Ames and commute to shopping, groceries, and campus. (Photograph copyright ©IADOT. All rights reserved.)

Four

PEOPLE AND INSTITUTIONS

Like all towns and cities, Ames is a product of its people and the institutions they created. Religious institutions, hospitals, schools, a vibrant Main Street, and involved civic organizations have all marked the progress of Ames from a town of sloughs to a diverse, 21st-century city. Aided by civic and cultural pioneers like Wallace Greeley, Neta Snook, Archie and Nancy Martin, and Farwell T. Brown, Ames has kept its vision fixed firmly on a better future that builds on the past. While the founding fathers did not always possess an enlightened, civic-minded spirit, by the late 1880s, Ames began to reflect the progressive attitude of the age and set a course of achievement and progress that it maintains today.

Three Ames institutions are captured in this photograph from around 1905. The familiar delivery wagon and team from Iowa State College stand in the foreground. Behind them, the passenger cars of the steam Dinkey are visible, and farther behind, to the right, is H.L. Munn & Son, an Ames family-owned business founded in 1891 and still in operation as H.L. Munn Lumber Company. (FTBPA.)

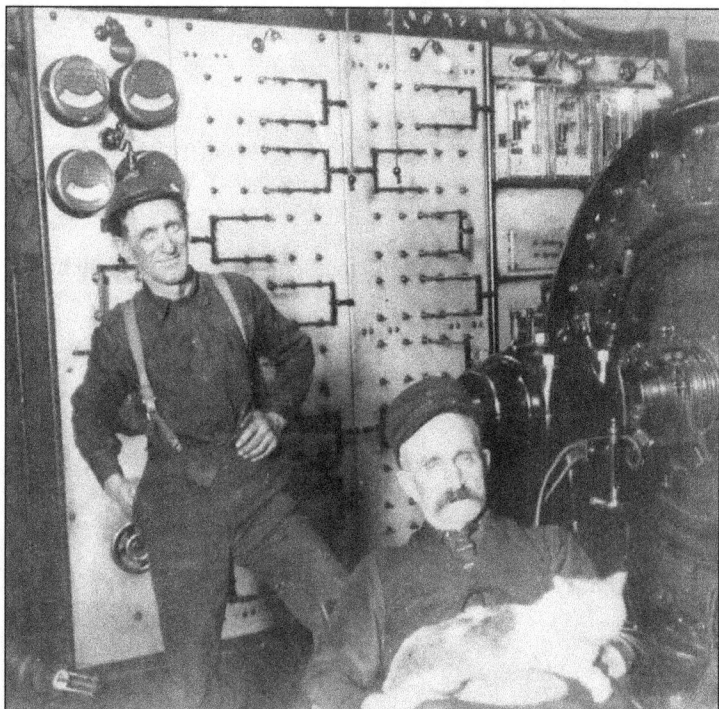

Electricity came to Ames in 1896 when citizens voted to build a municipal power plant. The original Ames Municipal Light Plant sat on the site of the current power plant at the east end of Main Street. The original plant was small and employed few staff. Pictured here around 1900 is plant engineer Charles Haverly (holding cat), father-in-law of Ben Nelson, founder of Nelson Electric. (Courtesy of Nelson Electric.)

Tall, big-hearted, and friendly, Henry "Hank" Wilkinson was one of Ames's most well-known citizens in the late 19th century. He began service as the conductor on the Dinkey in 1892, and the newspapers turned him into a local celebrity. He left the Dinkey for employment at Iowa State College in 1907 and was beloved by students, faculty, and townspeople until his untimely death in 1914. (Special Collections, ISU Library.)

An Interurban streetcar rolls past the Odd Fellows Lodge building, with its magnificent cornice, around 1910. Many early Ames luminaries were members of the Odd Fellows Lodge, pledging themselves to altruistic advancement of their community and fellow men. The building, constructed in 1901, burned in 1917 and was replaced with a less-grand structure, which serves as the American Legion Hall (AHS.)

Congregational Church, Ames, Iowa.

The Congregational Church housed the first congregation formed in Ames. Oakes Ames himself donated the church bell to the original structure in 1865. This photograph, taken in about 1915, shows the second church on the site of the original at Sixth Street and Kellogg Avenue. Ames now boasts many other Christian denominations as well as the Ames Jewish Congregation (1962) and the Darul Aqum Islamic Center (1985). (FTBPA.)

Wallace Greeley, the nephew of abolitionist Horace Greeley, was a New York native. He served as a captain in the 20th US Colored Infantry from 1863 to 1865 and, in 1866, moved to Ames, where he was a farmer, banker, and benefactor in his community. Known around Ames as "Captain Greeley," he figured prominently in almost every improvement in Ames between 1886 and his death in 1917. Greeley was a shrewd businessman, so when the city council raised the tax assessment on his personal property from $235 to $5,000 in 1886, he complained. Miraculously, he was able to get his personal assessment reduced from $5,000 to its original level of $235 even when other Downtown merchants were stuck paying higher taxes. The editors of the *Ames Intelligencer* told readers that Greeley achieved this reduction in his assessment through "falsehood, misrepresentation, intimidation, and cheek in bulldozing the council." "Let it not be forgotten," the paper continued, that "the richest man in Ames has only $235 worth of personal property." (FTBPA.)

With a land donation from Wallace and Mary Greeley and a $10,000 grant from Andrew Carnegie, Ames built a small but well-used public library in 1904. The original plot of land for the Ames Public Library is typical of sites for early 20th-century libraries: a building site on a corner, at the edge of a commercial district, bordering a residential area, in this case, the lot on the corner of Douglas Avenue and Sixth Street. One of the state's premier architectural firms, Hallett & Rawson (which became part of Proudfoot & Bird) designed the building. The 1904 Carnegie library is a split-story composition of brick facade and Bedford-stone foundation in a common Beaux-Arts design that reflects the prevailing civic style of the time. In 1908, a small addition to the library (above, right rear), also designed by Hallett & Rawson, expanded the interior space slightly. This addition was removed in 1940 when a second, more extensive library expansion occurred (below, right). (AHS.)

Fires posed a significant problem in early Ames. In the late 1880s, three fires destroyed most of the business district. In 1891, the new water tower enabled firefighting, and after the turn of the century, Ames organized a proper fire department, housed today in three stations. In this pre-1915 photograph, members of the volunteer fire company stand before the old town hall. (FTBPA.)

By the 1910s, the 1880s town hall was obsolete. In 1915, the city constructed a new municipal building, shown here in 1921. This building served as the administrative center of Ames until the city's continued growth required a move to a larger facility in 1990. At that time, city hall moved to the newly renovated 1938 high school building, now listed in the National Register of Historic Places. (AHS.)

When Mary Greeley died in 1914, her husband, Wallace Greeley, decided to build a hospital for the city of Ames in her memory. Construction on the three-story Mary Greeley Memorial Hospital was completed in 1916, and Greeley gave the hospital to the city. Today, a much-expanded facility, Mary Greeley Medical Center, is a major regional care provider in central Iowa. (AHS.)

World War I saw the entry of women into the workforce in jobs traditionally held by men. Julia Loughlan, pictured here in 1917, took a job as train caller at the Ames depot, becoming the only woman train caller and stationmaster in the country. In 1919, when the railway tried to phase her out, the Ames Chamber of Commerce convinced the Chicago & North Western to keep her. (FTBPA.)

Neta Snook, pictured here in 1921, moved with her family to Ames in 1915. She had always wanted to learn to fly, and though a series of events delayed her licensure, accounts say she became Iowa's first licensed female pilot in 1919. In 1920, after moving to California, she became the first woman to run a commercial airfield, Kinner Field, where, in 1921, she taught Amelia Earhart to fly. (AHS.)

Aviation pioneer J. Herman Banning, shown here in about 1927, moved to Ames in 1919 to study electrical engineering at Iowa State College. Leaving college after only a year, he took up aviation and became the first African American flyer to be licensed by the US Department of Commerce. Banning left Ames in 1929 to pursue his aviation career in California. (FTBPA.)

From the 1920s to the 1940s, Archibald "Archie" (left) and Nancy (right) Martin opened their home as lodging for African American students at Iowa State College. Unlike many colleges across the country, Iowa State admitted students of color and allowed them to take courses with white students. George Washington Carver graduated in 1894 as the lone African American, and it would be 20 more years before a second African American student graduated. Because the college required students of color to room together and so few attended Iowa State, most African American students were forced to live off campus. To provide housing for these students, Archie and three of his sons built a large, Craftsman-style house at 218 Lincoln Way (below) with room enough to take in lodgers. In 2004, Iowa State University named a new residence building Archie and Nancy Martin Hall to honor the generosity and sacrifice made by the couple. The Martin House, where so many African American students lodged, was designated an Ames Local Historic Landmark in 2009. (Both, FTBPA.)

The city's waterworks was founded in 1891, and a wooden water tower soon went up on Kellogg Avenue, followed by the installation of water mains and hydrants on Main Street. In 1927, the first water-filtration plant—still in service today, though much improved and expanded—was constructed to bring safe drinking water to Ames. A softening plant followed in 1931, shown in this 1935 photograph. (Photograph courtesy City of Ames.)

Ames had a lone town marshal from the late 1880s, but it was not until after 1900 that a proper police force was formed. In this photograph, police chief Bill Cure points to the new police cruiser that the department acquired in 1930. The Ames Police Department was housed in the municipal building until the move to the new city hall in 1990. (FTBPA.)

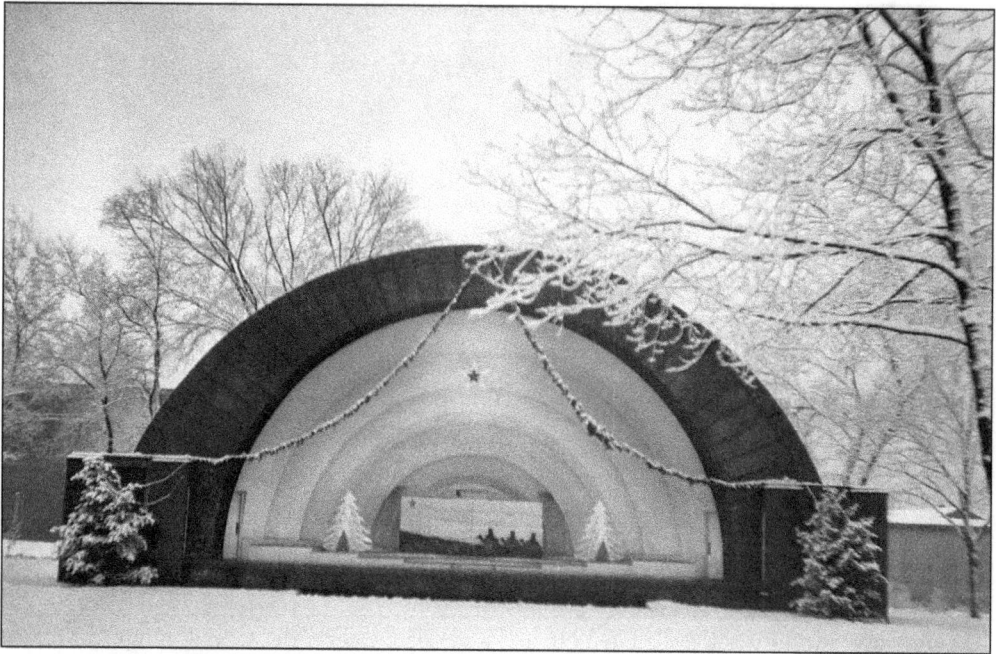

In 1935, Ames gained another cherished institution, the band shell in City Park, shown here decorated for the Christmas season that year. The band shell, from which the Band Shell Park National Register Historic District now takes its name, still hosts events each year, including summer concerts featuring the Ames Municipal Band. (FTBPA.)

After completing work on the Grand Avenue underpass, Ames contractor Ben Cole & Sons began work on a new city high school. This 1938 photograph shows the recently completed school in the 500 block of Clark Avenue, which replaced the 1912 high school building. Today, the 1938 school, listed in the National Register of Historic Places, serves as Ames City Hall and houses the police department, auditorium, and gymnasium. (FTBPA.)

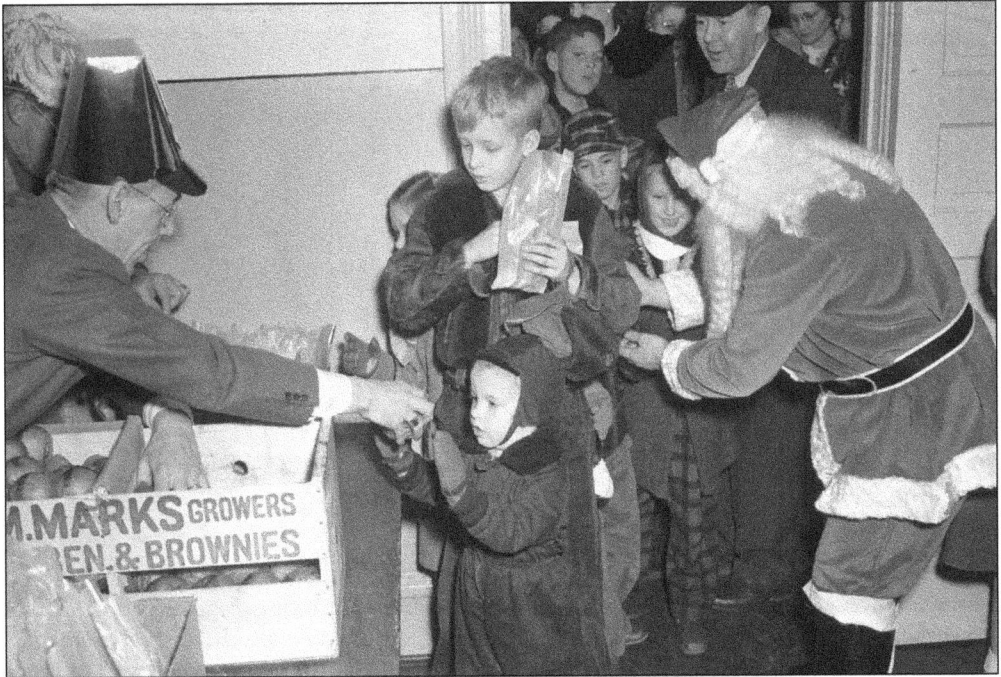

For many years at Christmas, the Ames Elks Club welcomed local children to a party with treats, entertainment, gifts, and a visit from Santa Claus. Handing out candy, nuts, and oranges in this 1948 photograph is Elks member Ed Kelley. Elks and their wives, as well as men from the city fire and police departments, participated in the festivities. (©*Ames Tribune*. All rights reserved.)

As service organizations like the Odd Fellows faded in the early 20th century, others, like Rotary, rose to take their place. Rotarians are part of an international service organization pledged to bringing business and professional leaders together to provide humanitarian services and build goodwill among all people. In 1947, the charter members of Ames Rotary were captured in this photograph. (FTBPA.)

Throughout the 1950s, Ames professional and benevolent organizations spearheaded the Christmas Basket Project, a community-wide effort that brought a bit of Christmas cheer to families in need. In this 1950 photograph, Ames Jaycees, Explorer Scouts from Ames High School, and members of the Ames Lions Club distribute baskets of toys and food. (©*Ames Tribune*. All rights reserved.)

Like the Christmas Basket Project, the Soroptimist service project in 1955 brought aid to a needy family. Local business and professional women chartered the Soroptimist Club of Ames in 1948. In 2008, that club celebrated its 60th anniversary as part of the larger organization Soroptimist International of the Americas, a service organization committed to improving the lives of women and girls around the world. (©*Ames Tribune*. All rights reserved.)

Significant expansion of the Ames Water Treatment Plant occurred in 1962, doubling its capacity, updating old infrastructure, and improving pumping power for the growing city. Smaller changes had brought new wells online, added extra office space in 1940, and introduced fluoridation in 1956, the date of this photograph. The original 1927 water-treatment plant will be decommissioned when a new facility is completed after 2014. (Photograph courtesy City of Ames.)

The City of Ames has been a leader in sustainability since the 1970s. In 1975, Ames became the first city in the country to open a waste-to-energy recovery plant. This photograph was taken during a tour of the Arnold O. Chantland Resource Recovery Plant in 1976. The plant's recovery system processes enough materials to produce electricity for 4,600 homes a year. (AHS.)

63

In 1980, lifelong Ames resident Farwell Tilden Brown helped to found the Ames Heritage Association to save and restore Hoggatt School, the first schoolhouse in Ames. As a third-generation member of two of Ames's oldest and most prominent families—the Tildens and the Browns—he became interested in the history of the community that his family had helped to build. His collection of photographs (the Farwell T. Brown Photographic Archive), his personal papers, recordings of his reminiscences, and his published works are among the best sources on the history of early Ames. After being named official historian for the city in 1986, Brown spent the next 24 years contributing to the public's understanding of Ames history. When he passed away in 2010, just shy of his 100th birthday, Ames lost a living piece of its history. The Ames Historical Society (formerly the Ames Heritage Association), in 2013, opened its newly remodeled and expanded Ames History Center, a tribute to historians with vision like Farwell Brown. (FTBPA.)

Five

DAILY LIFE AND LEISURE PASTIMES

Ames has always been a city that provides opportunities for citizens to enjoy life and share communal time with their neighbors. This Main Street Iowa community, which ranked number nine in *CNNMoney*'s top 100 best small cities in 2010, offers a high quality of daily life, with 36 parks, several shopping districts, an aquatic center, four golf courses, and boys' and girls' high school sports teams that bring home state championships. These leisure activities are not unique to 21st-century life in Ames. Citizens have enjoyed the benefits of municipal pools and parks, golf courses, social recreation, and spectator sports throughout the community's history. Leisure time in Ames has also meant joining organizations to share hobbies with like-minded individuals, as is the case with the Ames Garden Club; to pursue service to the community, as in organizations like Rotary, the Elks, or the Ames Community Chest (now United Way of Story County); or to learn about citizenship and responsibility with other young members of the Boy Scouts or Camp Fire USA (formerly Camp Fire Girls).

While Ames was officially a dry city for many years, students could always find a way around that policy. In 1911, an Iowa State College student sent this postcard, reporting that recently, "when the lights went out," a group of "naughty boys . . . went up town [for a] 'refreshment party.'" The wink inherent in the underlining and quotation marks suggests these young men were drinking something stronger than tea. (AHS.)

Chautauqua events were common in Ames from 1903 until the 1920s. Initially, large tents provided the venue, but those gave way to this auditorium, built in 1912 on ground now part of the municipal cemetery. Notables like Billy Sunday, William Jennings Bryan, and Booker T. Washington spoke at Ames Chautauqua meetings. The auditorium, sold to the Ames School District in 1927, was relocated and became the high school field house. (FTBPA.)

In this image from about 1912, the Ames High School girls' basketball team poses for a group photograph. In 1896, Clara Baer wrote rules for girls' six-on-six basketball that were widely adopted. Six-on-six ball remained the norm in Iowa until 1993, when Iowa became the second-to-last state in the nation to end the tradition; only Oklahoma played the sport longer (until 1995). (AHS.)

Football grew in popularity throughout the 1890s, but by 1905, when the sport's brutality resulted in 18 deaths and 180 injuries in college games, its future looked grim. That year, the Iowa High School Athletic Association banned its member schools from playing football, and it did not lift the ban until 1908. Four seasons later, in 1913, Ames High School's football team was photographed playing the West High team. (AHS.)

In this photograph, Ames Camp Fire Girls practice their camping skills. Iowa State College hosted the first national training course for Camp Fire leaders outside New York in 1914, but Ames's Camp Fire records begin only in 1916. In 1925, William and Myrtle Gaessler helped the Ames Camp Fire District Council select a site for a permanent camping facility, Camp Canwita, on land donated by Walter Grove. (FTBPA.)

The Collegian Theatre, once one of the finest examples of Art Deco in the Midwest, occupied the western end of Main Street from 1937 until 1975, when its facade was stripped and the building's shell became part of the US Bank building to the east. The Collegian got its name when 14-year-old Norma Jean Ross submitted the moniker to a naming contest sponsored by the Ames Theatre Company. (FTBPA.)

For over eight decades, Carr's Pool (seen here in the late 1930s) served the citizens of Ames as a place for recreation to beat the summer heat. Reuben Emmet "Dad" Carr built the pool in 1926 when Ames failed to pass a bond issue for a municipal pool. Prior to that time, swimmers used the Skunk River for recreation when the river had enough water and was not in flood. Carr's Pool prided itself on the purity of its water—a pleasant change from the river—and touted its "sanitary swimming pool" where kids could "swim in drinking water" that had been "scientifically treated." Families could also enjoy the "delightful picnic grounds" located "in a pleasing setting on the bank of Skunk River." Thousands of Ames children learned to swim at Carr's Pool, which remained family operated until 1973, when the City of Ames purchased it and changed the name to Carr Pool. Despite efforts to save the pool, it was razed in 2012 in the wake of construction of the new Furman Aquatic Center. (Both, FTBPA.)

LINCOLN WAY AT CAMPUSTOWN

By the 1940s, Campustown boasted a thriving commercial district with grocery stores, restaurants, druggists, two movie theaters, jewelry stores, banks, and clothiers—all the typical Downtown fare. The Champlin store building, the first brick building in Campustown, still anchors the 2400 block of Lincoln Way in this 1941 photograph, but Campus Drug now occupies the ground floor. In 1938, Joe Gerbracht's Ames Theatre Company had constructed a second movie house, the

70

Varsity, to join the already popular Ames Theatre on Lincoln Way. The area served students and residents of west Ames for many years until development farther west drew many businesses to migrate to new venues. Redevelopment of the 2400 block of Lincoln Way by Kingland Systems in 2014 brought the demolition of most of the buildings in this picture. (AHS.)

The women in this photograph won the league at Homewood Golf Course in 1949. In 1951, Ames citizens voted down a referendum to authorize the city to purchase Homewood. A similar vote passed in 1967, however, and women's golf leagues now play at Homewood Municipal Golf Course as well as at Coldwater Golf Links, the Ames Golf and Country Club, and Veenker Memorial Golf Course. (©*Ames Tribune*. All rights reserved.)

Before the construction of the Ames/Iowa State University Ice Arena in 2001, Ames children skated on outdoor rinks like this one at Brookside Park, pictured in 1955. Today, the only skaters at Brookside are those who use the Ames Skatepark, the skateboarding facility across Sixth Street from the former skating-rink site. (©*Ames Tribune*. All rights reserved.)

Like cities across the nation, Ames suffered from the effects of polio until Dr. Jonas Salk isolated a vaccine for the disease in 1952. The vaccine was declared safe and effective in April 1955. In this 1956 photograph, Ames parents and children line up outside McFarland Clinic on Fifth Street to await the vaccine. (©*Ames Tribune*. All rights reserved.)

By 1956, flooding had been a part of life in Ames for so long that these drivers did not even hesitate to brave the waters flowing across South Duff Avenue. Today, barricades would block the street, and motorists would be advised by National Weather Service protocol to "turn around don't drown." Of course, in 1956, the safety watchwords were "duck and cover." (©*Ames Tribune*. All rights reserved.)

Main Street businesses not only provided goods for daily life in Ames; they also provided entertainment for window shoppers. The inset entryways and large display windows typical of Ames's commercial architecture from the 1920s to the 1950s welcomed interested buyers and wishful thinkers. In this photograph, young consumers' faces are glued to a toy-store window as Christmas 1957 approaches. (©*Ames Tribune*. All rights reserved.)

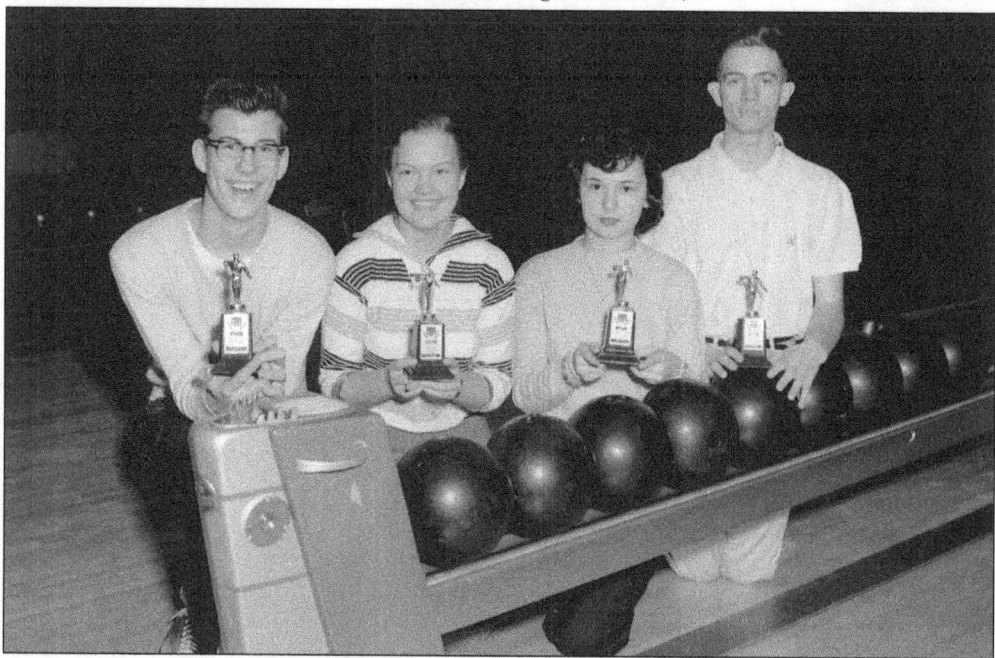

For good, clean fun, Ames kids like these 1958 trophy winners could hone their bowling skills. By the 1920s, Ames already had a bowling alley at the east end of Main Street. The location of the alley has changed over the decades, but the sport still maintains a place in community recreation, alongside laser tag and arcade games at Ames Perfect Games. (©*Ames Tribune*. All rights reserved.)

Even in 1958, not all kids were interested in having clean fun bowling. As is the case in many college towns, alcohol use provided a means of entertainment for both young people and their elders. This day-in-the-life photograph provides a sense of the amount of alcohol confiscated by the Ames Police Department. Today, the Ames police still handle alcohol-related offenses all too often. (©*Ames Tribune*. All rights reserved.)

In 1976, a new theater company joined ACTORS on the Ames drama scene. The Ames Women's Theater was founded specifically to allow more women to express their theatrical talents. The company attracted participants from both the Ames and Iowa State University communities and produced plays that offered multiple good roles for women or focused on women's issues and lives, though men were also part of the company. (AHS.)

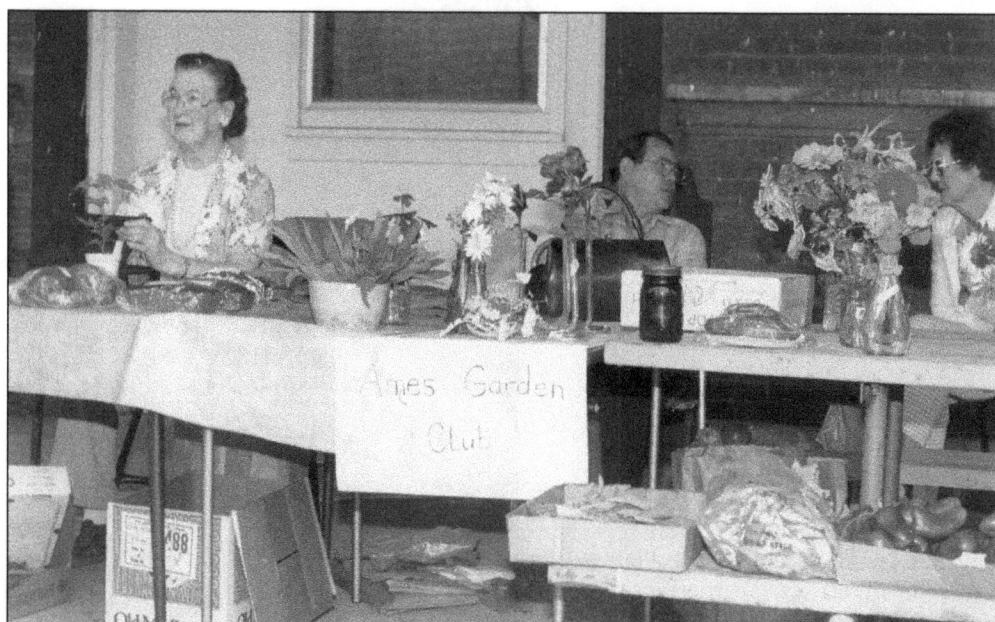

Ames Garden Club members sell flowers at the old Chicago & North Western depot in this 1981 photograph. When first chartered in 1923, the Ames Garden Club was a joint venture of Ames residents and the Iowa State College Botany and Horticulture Departments. Today, the club is active in local, state, and national activities and educational programs and still holds an annual plant sale at Reiman Gardens. (FTBPA.)

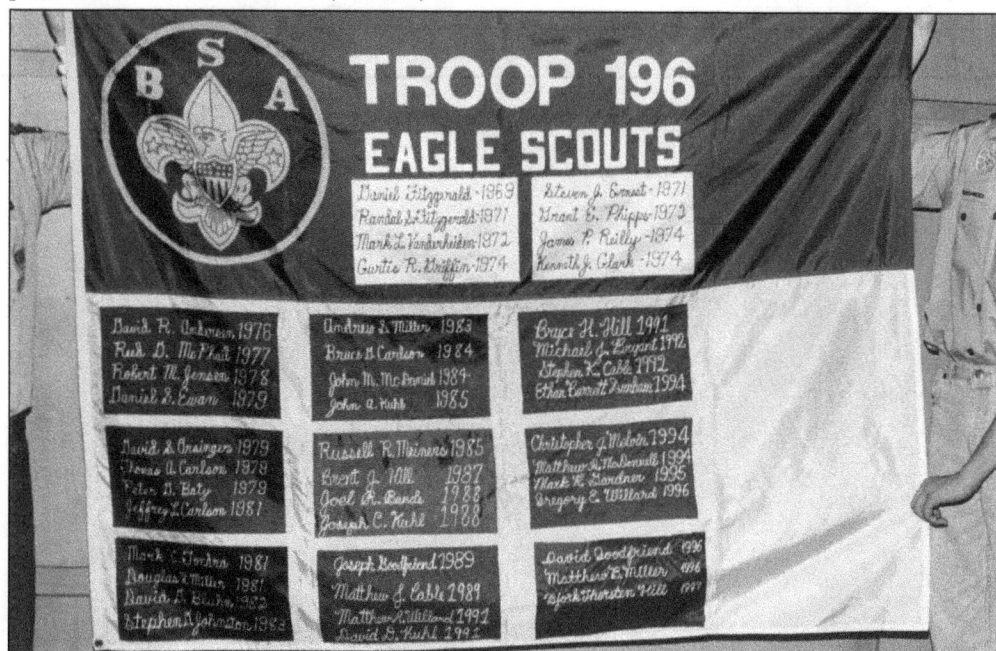

In this 1997 photograph, scouts from Ames Troop 196 proudly display a banner containing the names of all 35 Eagle Scouts from the troop since its founding in the 1960s. Scouting began in Ames soon after the Boy Scouts of America were founded in 1910, and thousands of boys have enjoyed scouting activities in the community over the years. (FTBPA.)

Six

THE CITY, THE STATE, AND THE NATION

With a major research university, a transportation hub, and the home for the Iowa State Highway Commission all within its city limits, Ames, throughout its 150 years, has been more involved with the state of Iowa than have some other municipalities. The community has also made its mark on the national scene. It is the home of the National Animal Disease Center, the largest animal-disease center in the United States, and has served as the headquarters for nationally known corporations like Collegiate Manufacturing and Hach Chemical. During World War II, scientists at Iowa State College developed the most efficient process to produce high-purity uranium metal in large quantities for the Manhattan Project, and Ames Laboratory, a national laboratory of the US Department of Energy, still engages in cutting-edge research that attracts the attention of the international scientific community. But Ames has also drawn political and social attention to the heart of Iowa. The list of notable visitors includes entertainers, evangelists, military leaders, governors, heads of state, and presidents.

On February 12, 1908, six cars representing four nations began the grueling ordeal of the road race from New York to Paris that took them west across the nation and then across Asia, Siberia, and Europe, to finally reach Paris in July. Here, the French car, the Moto Bloc, moves up the Boone Street (Lincoln Way) hill, lined with sycamore trees, by the Iowa State campus. (FTBPA.)

Nationally known evangelist William Ashley "Billy" Sunday, pictured in 1908, was born in Ames in 1862 and returned often to preach. Before becoming an evangelist and ordained Presbyterian minister, he played professional baseball for two Chicago White Stockings pennant-winning teams. Sunday used his fame as a baseball player to bring in large audiences for revival meetings like his first, held in 1897 in Garner, Iowa. (AHS.)

In 1910, former US president Theodore Roosevelt stopped in Ames on a trip across the country in anticipation of his run for another term in office in 1912. The popular former president was met by a reception committee of about 5,000 enthusiastic residents. Ames mayor Parley Sheldon (hand raised, at right) introduced Roosevelt (standing left of Sheldon) to the crowd at the Ames depot. (FTBPA.)

The Hog Cholera Research Station, pictured here in 1915, moved to Ames in 1905 and was the forerunner to the National Animal Disease Center. In 1907, Iowa State College alumnus Dr. W.B. Niles, along with Drs. M. Dorset and C.N. McBryde, developed an anti–hog cholera serum in these buildings. The City of Ames demolished the buildings in 2013 to make way for a new water-treatment facility. (FTBPA.)

In the autumn of 1915, race-car-driver-turned-actress Anita King became the first woman to drive across the country. She stopped in Ames on her way from Los Angeles to New York, and George Bates snapped this picture as her car stood across the street from the Bates Bakery at 130 Main Street. (FTBPA.)

In March 1916, Iowa State College welcomed former US president William Howard Taft to campus. On three separate days, President Taft spoke in State Gymnasium to large audiences of residents, students, war veterans, and state and local dignitaries on the topics "Our World Relations," "Military and Naval Defenses of the United States," and "The Duties of Citizenship." (FTBPA.)

In 1901, the Iowa State College Engineering Division began experimental work in highway engineering, which led to establishment of the Iowa Highway Commission at Ames in 1904. Testing of road materials, like that being done on the bridge crossbeam in this photograph from about 1926, led to steady improvement of the nation's road system, facilitating long-distance automobile travel. (Photograph copyright ©IADOT. All rights reserved.)

Pictured in 1944, Earl Howard, of Ames's Howard Flying Service, was chosen in September 1940 to head the Civilian Flight Training Program. This program, organized under the joint auspices of Iowa State College and the federal government, would prepare pilots for what some feared was a coming war. After December 7, 1941, the newly renamed War Training Service Program produced pilots to aid the war effort. (FTBPA.)

Increasing demand for pilots led to the need for more Howard Flying Service hangars, which were located at the new Ames Municipal Airport with its two runways completed in 1944. Earl Howard was the first manager of that airport, built in southern Ames west of US Highway 69. In this photograph, the Flying Service instructors and staff stand proudly before their aircraft and the new hangars. (FTBPA.)

In 1944, Collegiate Manufacturing received the Army-Navy E (Excellence) Award for the quality and quantity of the company's contributions to the war effort (making raincoats and ponchos for the troops). In this photograph, representatives from the US Army and Navy flank employees and officers of Collegiate Manufacturing. Iowa State College received a similar Army-Navy E Banner in 1945 for excellence in metallurgical research supporting the war effort. (FTBPA.)

During World War II, this temporary building on the Iowa State College campus was known as "Little Ankeny" after the ordnance works in Ankeny, Iowa. Here, physical chemistry professors Harley Wilhelm and Frank Spedding, along with their team of scientists and students, developed an efficient process for refining uranium for the Manhattan Project. More than two million pounds of pure uranium were produced between 1942 and 1946. (Special Collections, ISU Library).

In the fall of 1946, veterans returning from World War II flooded campuses across the country, creating a need for affordable housing. Iowa State College met this need by building Pammel Court, the housing subdivision seen here around 1946, using government surplus barracks and trailers. This group of buildings provided student apartments for over 50 years until the last unit was razed in 2004. (FTBPA.)

In 1950, Iowa State College physical chemistry professors Harley Wilhelm (center) and Frank Spedding (right) gave a tour of the college's nuclear-research facility to Iowa governor William Beardsley (left). The first research building constructed for the Ames Laboratory, the Metallurgy Building (now Wilhelm Hall), had been completed in 1949. A second building, the Research Building (now Spedding Hall), was completed in 1951. (©*Ames Tribune*. All rights reserved.)

In September 1956, Pres. Dwight Eisenhower and his wife, Mamie, visited Ames on a campaign swing. An estimated 20,000 people came out to greet the president during his brief, 20-minute stop in Ames. The importance of this event might be gauged by the turnout; at the time, Ames had a population of around 23,000. (©*Ames Tribune*. All rights reserved.)

Ames citizens rang in the New Year in 1956 by welcoming home the Iowa State Cyclone men's basketball team, which had just won the Big Seven Conference championship in Kansas City, Kansas. A crowd, including the Ames High School band, greeted the triumphant team's bus at city hall on January 3. In 2014, the Cyclones returned from Kansas City as the Big Twelve champions. (©*Ames Tribune*. All rights reserved.)

Growing out of the Manhattan Project work completed by the Spedding-Wilhelm team, the federal government's Ames Laboratory moved into its first purpose-built home at Iowa State College in 1949. In 1958, the date of this photograph showing Ames Laboratory rare earth metals experimentation, the federal government approved nearly $6 million to construct two new Atomic Energy Commission buildings in Ames for research on rare earth metals. (©*Ames Tribune*. All rights reserved.)

In September 1959, Soviet premier Nikita Khrushchev visited Ames and the Iowa State University campus to open dialogue on how to help Soviet farmers increase yields to better feed their people. The visit to Ames was part of a 12-day cross-country tour of the United States that ended in a summit with President Eisenhower at Camp David, Maryland. (Special Collections, ISU Library.)

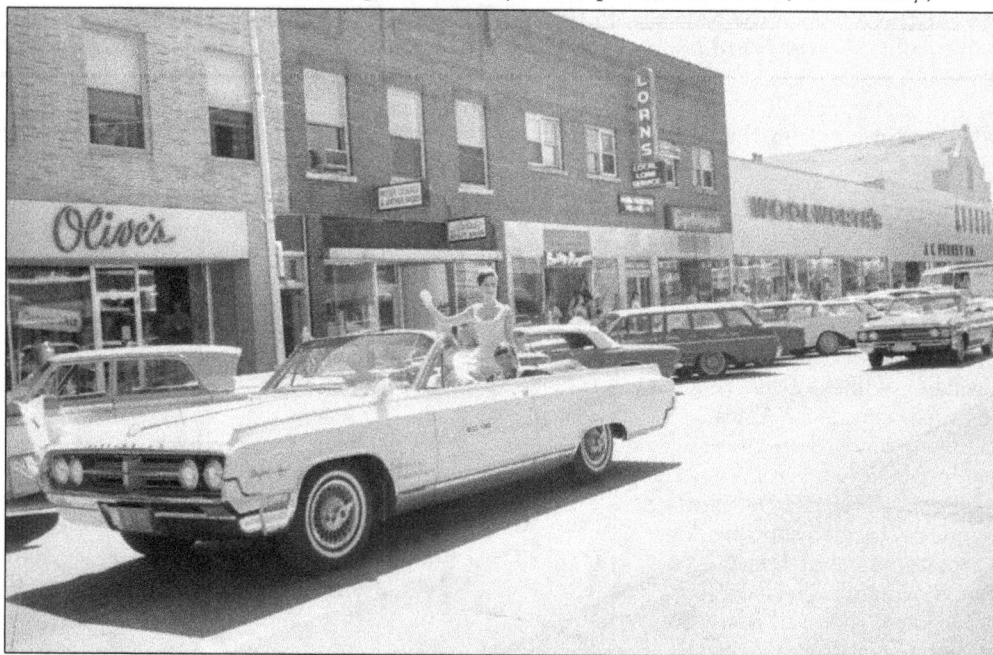

Ames's own Carol Lyn Johnson, Miss Ames 1964, was crowned Miss Iowa that same year. In July, her hometown honored her with a parade and a reception sponsored by the Ames Jaycees. Mayor Pearle DeHart gave Johnson the key to the city after her trip down Main Street, shown here. (©*Ames Tribune*. All rights reserved.)

On October 15, 1976, as part of his presidential campaign, Pres. Gerald Ford delivered a speech at the Iowa State Center. At the very opening of his speech the president misspoke, saying that he was glad to be at "Ohio . . . uh, Iowa State." The dignitaries seated behind President Ford are, from left to right, W. Robert Parks, Robert D. Ray, and Lee Fellinger. The others are unidentified. (Special Collections, ISU Library.)

On May 29, 1976, Elvis Presley, "the King of Rock and Roll," brought his tour to Ames. He performed before a sellout crowd in Hilton Coliseum. The King gave a good show, but he was not what he had been. As one reviewer described the 1976 concert event, "Elvis, F-A-T, but fun." (©*Ames Tribune*. All rights reserved.)

In November 1984, Iowa's farm economy nearly collapsed under debt accrued in the 1970s, declining foreign export of farm commodities, and the decade's low farm prices. Awareness of the crisis among the general public was poor until February 1985, when the National Farmers Organization, the Iowa State Extension Service, and Iowa State University sponsored the National Crisis Action Rally at Hilton Coliseum (above). The rally, attended by delegates from 20 states and from around Iowa, brought national attention to the issue. The 15,000 attendees arrived in buses, by automobile, and on tractors (below) in an attempt to draw the attention of national media and lawmakers. (Both, FTBPA.)

Seven

LOCAL EVENTS OF NOTE

Like all communities, Ames has seen its share of significant events, accidents, tragedies, and natural disasters. Because Ames did not have a proper fire department until after 1900, fires were often a fear in the early years. Ames's business district burned three times in the 1880s, and even after the establishment of modern firefighting in the community, fires occasionally broke out Downtown and devastated businesses. Residents have also seen more than their share of floods. Since its founding in the flood plain of two significant watersheds, Ames has weathered floods that have caused millions of dollars in damage. Railway accidents, bombings, and blizzards all have marked the years of Ames's existence. Bad times, however, are only part of the story; Ames has also celebrated community and nation, sometimes turning simple, everyday things like bond drives, back-to-school enthusiasm, and safety-awareness campaigns into noteworthy occasions. The Fourth of July and Veteran's Day bring annual parades, while Iowa State University's VEISHEA celebration each spring joins town to university.

In 1898, the Loughran Machine Company, founded by Ames pioneer Edmund Loughran, entered this float in the annual Fourth of July parade. Here, the float, advertising McCormick farm implements, is being pulled down Onondaga (Main) Street past a group of Civil War veterans (foreground). Loughran Machine was located at the east end of Onondaga and later became a storage building for Munn Lumber Company. (FTBPA.)

As a busy transportation hub, Ames has experienced its share of rail accidents. The one in this photograph occurred in November 1907 when a Fort Dodge, Des Moines & Southern streetcar packed with 40 passengers ran through a signal crossing the Chicago & North Western main line and was struck by an oncoming freight train. Miraculously, no one was killed, but most of the passengers were injured, some seriously. (FTBPA.)

90

The Odd Fellows, an international society pledged to humanitarian efforts in local communities, was a popular fraternal organization in the late 19th and early 20th centuries. The handsome Odd Fellows building, constructed in 1901, stood taller than any other edifice on Main Street before it was destroyed by fire in 1917. Rebuilt to almost the same height the following year, it now houses the Ames American Legion Hall. (FTBPA).

Heavy rains in the spring of 1918 caused a memorable flood that washed out the automobile bridge over Squaw Creek on Lincoln Way. In this photograph, downed powerlines and the washed-out roadway make it impossible for travelers coming from the college (background, right) to get to Downtown Ames. (FTBPA.)

In this photograph taken at the time of the 1918 flood, the Fort Dodge, Des Moines & Southern streetcar carefully crosses its bridge between campus and Downtown. The wreckage of the footbridge that ran parallel to the Interurban tracks can be seen at left. (FTBPA.)

Since 1875, when Ames first honored its veterans, the city has recognized their sacrifices to protect the country's freedom. This photograph shows the veterans parade in 1919 honoring those who had fought in all wars, but particularly World War I. Today, Ames has a veterans' memorial on the corner of Grand Avenue and Fifth Street that honors veterans' military service to this nation. (FTBPA.)

As a land-grant institution, Iowa State College was required to maintain and educate a corps of cadets to help in national defense during times of need. While the college had a corps of cadets from the beginning, it built an armory much later, in 1920. On December 16, 1922, that armory burned to the ground. The structure was rebuilt and still stands today. (FTBPA.)

In the late 19th and early 20th centuries, May Day festivals heralded the coming of spring in communities across the country. Ames schoolgirls and college women celebrated the festival annually in the 1910s and 1920s. This photograph shows Central Junior High School students dancing around a Maypole during a 1923 May Day celebration. (FTBPA).

Iowa State College instituted the VEISHEA festival in 1922 to help with student recruitment, and it became a spring celebration that drew townspeople and college community together. In this photograph, future Ames historian Farwell Brown, dressed as Uncle Sam, rides a penny-farthing bicycle in the 1934 VEISHEA parade. As of 2013, VEISHEA was the largest student-run celebration in the country. (FTBPA.)

Main Street shines brightly in the night in this October 1929 photograph. The newly installed Electrolier lighting system on Main Street improved on the original electric lights and enhanced evening shopping hours for Downtown businesses. By the late 1920s, traffic was already becoming a problem in Downtown Ames; the well-lit streets helped pedestrians to walk more safely at night. (FTBPA.)

The issue of heavy traffic in the 1930s was partially solved by the completion of the Grand Avenue underpass in 1938 (shown here). The railroads and street traffic no longer had to compete for time at grade crossings. The highway engineers faced significant challenges in building three bridges for heavily trafficked railroad lines and streets. The Interurban bridge in the foreground was later taken down. (FTBPA.)

Between 1930 and 1940, Ames's population grew 22 percent, and by the mid-1930s, it had outgrown the Carnegie library. Plans began for an addition designed by local architects Allen Kimball and Charles Bowers, which opened in 1940. This expansion during the Depression indicates Ames's economic stability even as other Iowa communities were faring poorly; between 1921 and 1940, there were 80 Iowa communities that voted to have libraries, but only seven library buildings were actually constructed. (Courtesy of Michael Thole.)

Ames in the early 1940s was at the center of several large storms. On November 11, 1940, the Armistice Day Blizzard dropped up to 27 inches of snow on Iowa, Minnesota, Wisconsin, Nebraska, and Michigan, leaving a number of hunters and thousands of waterfowl dead. Ames got several inches of blowing snow that made travel perilous, but that was nothing compared to the 13 inches of blowing snow that came the third week of December that year. On New Year's Day 1942, another major blizzard hit Ames, trapping a *Life* magazine photographer and his camera in town. The magazine reported that 24 inches of the "white stuff" had fallen in 24 hours. In these major snow events, blowing and drifting made moving around town very difficult, as these 1940 photographs illustrate. (Both, FTBPA.)

Torrential rains came to Ames in May 1944, leaving 8.21 inches in 24 hours and causing flooding the *Ames Daily Tribune* called the "worst in history." Squaw Creek (seen here), the Skunk River, and College Creek all burst their banks. Veenker Memorial Golf Course was flooded, as were the basements of many Campustown and Downtown businesses, the Grand Avenue underpass, and houses all over town. (FTBPA.)

In this 1951 photograph, Ames Automobile Dealers Association members joined together at Band Shell Park with Ames police chief Orville Erickson (far left) and state trooper Mel Hove (far right) to promote safe driving. At the safety check-up, 15 Ames children and adults won prizes. (©*Ames Tribune*. All rights reserved.)

The retirement of Ames city manager John H. Ames in October 1953 marked the end of the longest single managerial term to that point. John H. Ames, shown in this 1930 photograph, served the community for 26 years. He oversaw the laying of concrete pavement and sewer lines citywide and construction of the band shell, municipal airport, new power plant, and water filtration plant. (©*Ames Tribune*. All rights reserved.)

Ames opened a new city landfill site near the municipal airport in 1954. The covering of trash with layers of earth provided an early means for the city to combat pollution, as the refuse no longer needed to be burned for disposal. The Ames Resource Recovery Plant, built in 1975, was the next step toward sustainability. (©*Ames Tribune*. All rights reserved.)

In 1954, the Ames Public Library celebrated 50 years of service. For half of those years, Letha Davidson (second from right) held the post of library director. Davidson presided over an unparalleled period of expansion and growth of the library, and her contributions including spearheading the 1940 expansion project. She served as director for 34 years, retiring in 1963. (©*Ames Tribune*. All rights reserved.)

Even a common occurrence like going back to school could be turned into a notable event. In 1957, J. C. Penney celebrated its golden jubilee and the return to school by hosting a movie party at the Collegian Theatre. In this photograph, a group of enthusiastic children parade down Main Street past radio station KASI, which had gone on the air in 1948. (©*Ames Tribune*. All rights reserved.)

By 1958, the old Lincoln Way bridge over Squaw Creek had become too narrow to properly serve the traffic flow. Over the course of many months, a new bridge was constructed in multiple stages to replace the old one. This photograph shows the new bridge shortly after the old had been dismantled. Mere weeks later, the project was threatened by another major flood. (©*Ames Tribune*. All rights reserved.)

Throughout the 1950s, traffic on US highways increased as more cars and trucks filled America's roadways. The Lincoln Highway (US 30) through Ames was no exception. By 1963, when this photograph was taken, the volume of traffic through Ames's Campustown business district was great enough that widening Lincoln Way to four lanes proved necessary. Only five years later, the state completed a US Highway 30 bypass south of town. (FTBPA.)

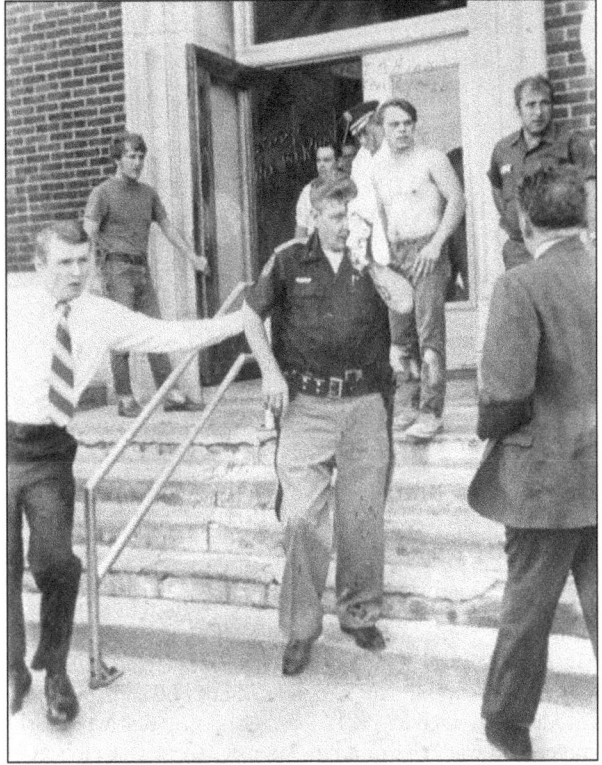

On May 22, 1970, a bomb was left by a basement window of the Ames Police Department, then housed in the Ames Municipal Building. The bomb contained 15 pounds of explosives, which heavily damaged the cell block, caused shockwaves up to six blocks away, and blew out windows over a wide area. There were no fatalities, but nine people were injured, and highway patrolman Charles Elliott (right) lost the use of his left eye. The Ames Municipal Building bomb was only one of four threatened or planted in central Iowa in early summer 1970. The bomber has never been apprehended. (Both, ©*Ames Tribune*. All rights reserved.)

The year 1970 also brought the long-awaited opening of a new and improved Elwood Drive (now University Boulevard) that could act as a gateway to Ames, bringing visitors directly from the new US Highway 30 bypass to Iowa State University via the impressive Iowa State Center, which now boasted an almost-complete James H. Hilton Coliseum (the 14,384-seat multipurpose arena scheduled to open in 1971). The reopening of Elwood drive as a four-lane boulevard rather than a gravel road was celebrated in August 1970 with a ribbon-cutting ceremony hosted by Ames mayor Staurt Smith (with megaphone) and Iowa State University president W. Robert Parks (left). The aerial photograph below demonstrates the truly monumental scale of both Hilton Coliseum and Elwood Drive; the small road (by comparison) in the background is the recently widened Lincoln Way, now dwarfed by the new construction. (Both, ©*Ames Tribune*. All rights reserved.)

Etta "Lee" Fellinger became Ames's first woman mayor in the 1976 election. Fellinger had previously served on the city council as the representative for Ames's second ward from 1968 to 1972. When she ran for the mayor's office in 1976, the Women's Movement was a strong force in American society, and the time was right for Ames to elect its first woman mayor. Similar forces were at work in mayoral races around the country, and Fellinger was photographed for the cover of *Family Weekly* with a group of women mayors at the National League of Cities conference. She must have gained the approval of the citizens of Ames; she was elected for a second term and served until 1979. Since Fellinger, Ames has had only one other woman mayor, Ann Campbell, who was reelected to a third term in office in 2013. (AHS.)

Another of Ames's noteworthy railroad mishaps occurred in April 1981 when empty hopper cars from a Chicago & North Western freight train jumped the tracks while traveling through Downtown. Several of the cars went over the rail of the bridge and ended up on Grand Avenue below. Fortunately, there were no fatalities. (FTBPA.)

In November 1987, Ames Stationers, a longtime Main Street business, suffered a severe fire, pictured here. The business, which had originally sold greeting cards, paper, and office supplies as the Ames News Stand, founded in 1912, lost the second story of its building, constructed in 1913 for the Ames Trust & Savings Bank. Ames Stationers reopened but, facing competition from big box stores, went out of business in 1995. (FTBPA.)

Eight

ONE COMMUNITY, 1964–2014

The 50 years since the Ames centennial in 1964 have brought growth and change. The city's population has more than doubled since 1960, bringing more ethnic diversity, widening gaps between economic groups, and increasing exposure to the ills of American society. Growth has added new national chains alongside familiar local businesses on Ames's thoroughfares, extending the business districts from Main Street and Campustown, making South Duff Avenue and West Lincoln Way booming development corridors, and bringing new commercial nodes to developing neighborhoods to the city's north and west. This expansion has necessitated an enhancement of city services and the CyRide public transport system, much of which has been accomplished since 1982 under the management of Ames's longest-serving city manager, Steven L. Schainker. Ames and Iowa State University have striven to build one community by encouraging and maintaining communication between university and city administrators, students, and permanent residents. But even as Ames has changed, some aspects of life have continued much as they were in the first century of the town's history. Ames remains a community that turns out for parades, rallies for celebrations, meets its sports teams returning home in victory or defeat, and honors its veterans. The Union Pacific Railroad runs over 50 freight trains through the heart of town on a daily basis; US Highways 30 and 69 still carry traffic to all parts of the country; and floods and fires continue to pose challenges to the vibrant city of the early 21st century.

In 1964, Ames celebrated its 100th year. The community produced a centennial history, performed a pageant about Ames, and sponsored a parade that wound several miles through neighborhoods and Downtown. Ames men honored the community's history by participating in the "Brothers of the Brush" beard contest. In this 1964 photograph, Ames insurance salesman and future mayor Frank "Ted" Tedesco sports an 1860s-style beard and centennial tie. (FTBPA.)

The Congregational Church was the first church to be built in Ames in the mid-1860s. During the centennial parade in 1964, the Congregationalists' float touted their pride of place as one of Ames's oldest religious institutions, proclaiming "First Church Services Held in R.R. Depot." A "congregation" of children seated on "pews" depicts a service before the construction of the church at Sixth Street and Kellogg Avenue. (FTBPA.)

Ames's centennial parade, held on September 12, 1964, featured a number of floats, bands, and groups marching. Among those organizations that participated, the Tama Indian tribe from Tama, Iowa, sponsored by the Ames Association of Independent Insurance Agents, marched in the parade to honor their Native American heritage. (©*Ames Tribune*. All rights reserved.)

Another entry in the centennial parade was the Templeton Saturn shown here. In 1948, Lloyd Templeton of Fort Madison, Iowa, built a car he called the Saturn because it supposedly ran rings around other automobiles. While several Saturns were built, they never caught on, in spite of Templeton's efforts and belief that his car would be the future of US automotive production. (©*Ames Tribune*. All rights reserved.)

107

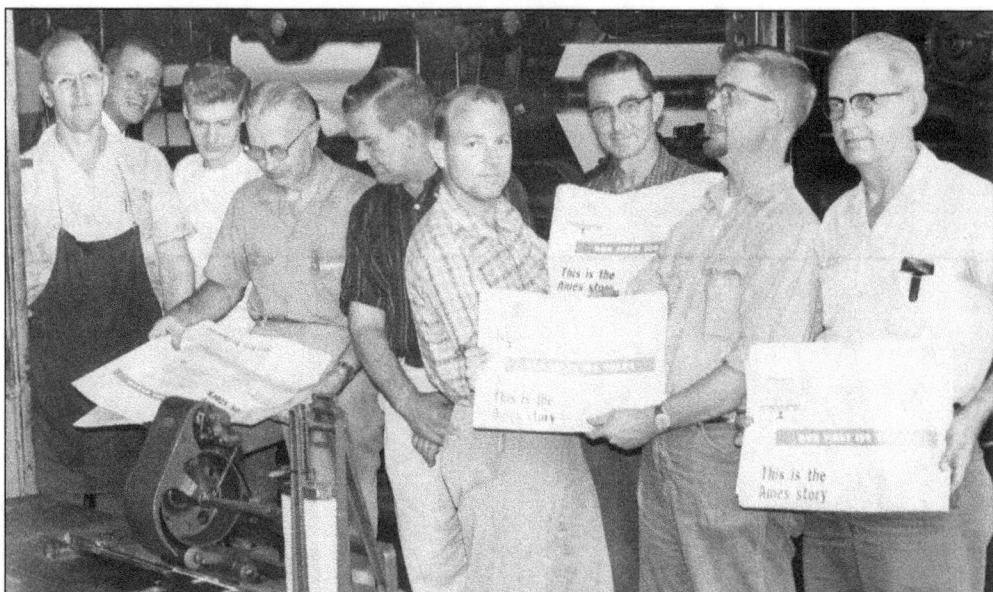

The *Ames Intelligencer*, the first newspaper in Ames, began publication in 1868. It was followed in 1892 by the *Ames Times*, which eventually purchased the *Intelligencer*. The *Ames Tribune* began publication in 1911 and merged with the *Times* in 1919 to become the *Ames Daily Tribune*. Today, the *Ames Tribune* provides news and commentary to all of Story County. In this 1964 photograph, *Tribune* staff display the newspaper's centennial edition. (AHS photograph, courtesy of Carol Cummings.)

In 1966, the Chicago & North Western Railroad removed its switching yard from the land immediately south of Main Street. Since Ames's founding, the yard had effectively divided the Downtown from light industry and less-expensive residential areas south of the tracks. With the removal of the switching yard, the city gained public spaces and parking for Downtown businesses. (©*Ames Tribune*. All rights reserved.)

In 1968, when this photograph was taken, Main Street was still the city's primary business district. Although the district lost stalwarts such as J. C. Penney, the Collegian Theatre, Woolworths, Younkers, and Bledsoe's in the next decades, new local businesses like Downtown Deli, Cooks Emporium, and Olde Main Brewing Company moved in to keep what is now the Main Street Cultural District vibrant. (©*Ames Tribune*. All rights reserved.)

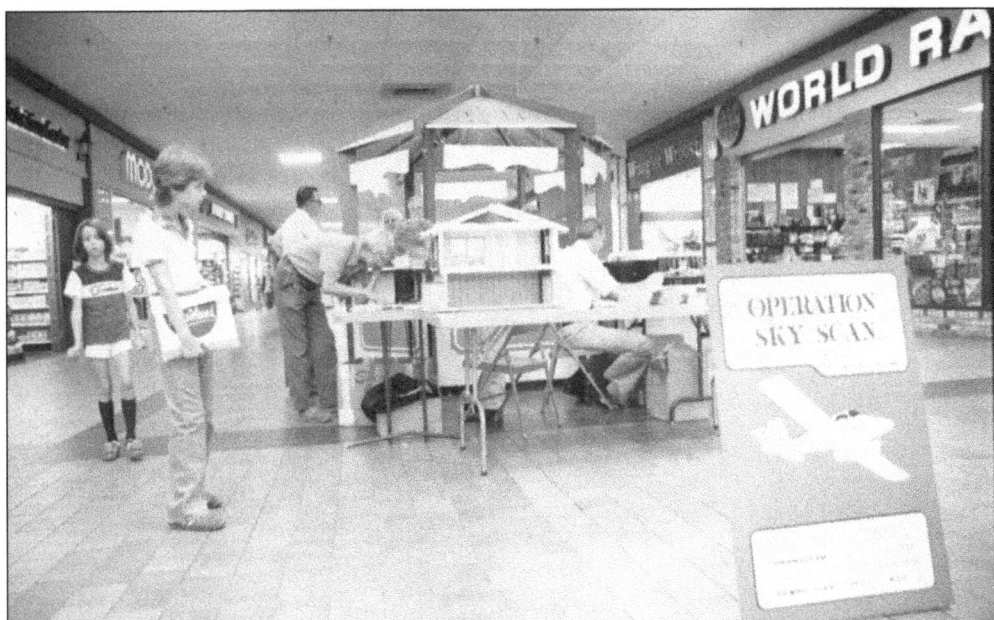

J. C. Penney and Younkers relocated from Main Street to the new North Grand Shopping Center (now North Grand Mall) in 1971 and 1972. The covered, climate-controlled mall offered a complete shopping experience, with 2,000 free parking spaces and over 400,000 square feet of floor space. This 1977 photograph shows the flexibility of the mall's atrium space, which is still used by temporary vendors. (©*Ames Tribune*. All rights reserved.)

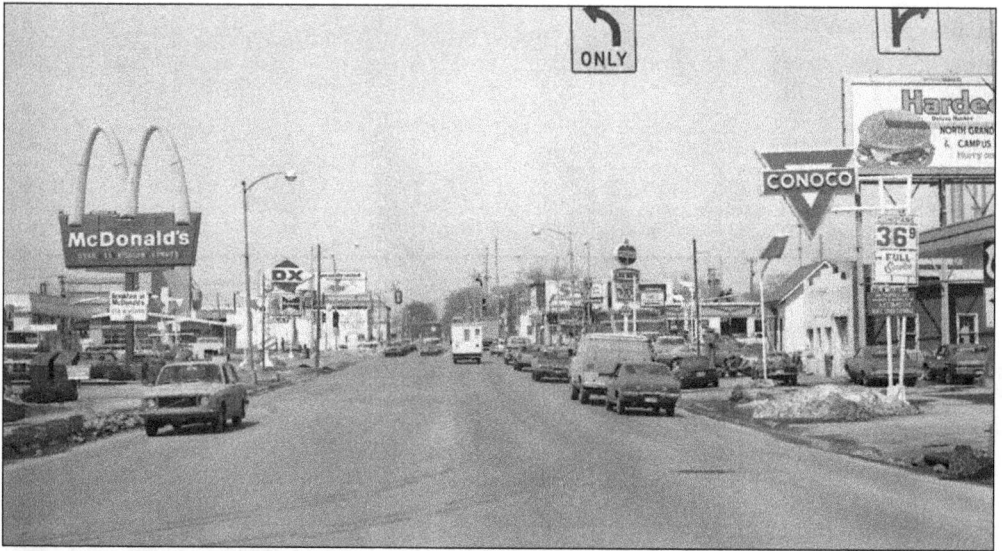

Following a 43.6 percent population increase throughout the 1960s, Ames began to attract national chains, including McDonald's and Hardee's. This 1973 photograph shows the early phase of the transition from local, highway-oriented businesses, like Jeff's Hamburgers and car dealerships, to chain stores, like Burger King, Perkins, Panera Bread Company, and Village Inn, which continue to dominate Duff Avenue and Lincoln Way today. (©*Ames Tribune*. All rights reserved.)

In 1911, the Ames Golf and Country Club was founded by 15 citizens on land south of the Iowa State College campus. The club survived at its original location until 1974, when it moved to its new 18-hole golf course north of town. To mark the event, club members, escorted by Ames police officers, drove their golf carts to the new course. (©*Ames Tribune*. All rights reserved.)

The mid-1970s saw a transition in Iowa State Cyclone football. The old stadium—Clyde Williams Field, built on campus between 1914 and 1915—had outlived its usefulness in an age of increased attendance and television revenue. These forces drove Iowa State University to begin construction in 1974 of a new stadium, located in the flood plain south of Iowa State Center. Many students, alumni, and supporters wished to name the stadium in honor of Jack Trice, Iowa State's first African American football player, who died of injuries sustained in his inaugural intercollegiate football game in 1924. However, the first game was played in 1975 on Jack Trice Field at Cyclone Stadium. The stadium itself was not renamed for Trice until 1997. The 1978 demolition of Clyde Williams Field marked the end of an era. (Both, ©*Ames Tribune*. All rights reserved.)

Memorial Day 1976 (the national bicentennial year), perhaps more than any previous Memorial Day, reminded Ames citizens of the foundation of the United States as a land of freedom and opportunity. For these values, thousands of men and women in the armed services sacrificed their lives. The above photograph shows the honor guard for the Memorial Day parade that year. Mayor Lee Fellinger, Ames's first woman mayor, delivered an address at the Ames Municipal Cemetery (below), commemorating the 101st anniversary of the first Ames Memorial Day parade. As the photograph demonstrates, many graves were covered with fresh flowers that day, including that of Capt. Charles Hamilton, the last Ames veteran of the Civil War, who passed away in 1941. (Both, FTBPA.)

In the US bicentennial year, Ames also rebuilt Main Street. Excavation like that seen in the photograph above resulted in a narrower street with a reduced traffic flow, making the Downtown area much more pedestrian friendly. Both this photograph and the one below show the evolution of Ames Main Street facades from Victorian style to streamlined, modern silhouettes. In the image below, which shows the northeast corner of Kellogg Avenue and Main Street, the China Center occupies a storefront in the Opera House Block built by Judge John L. Stevens and Professor Joseph L. Budd in 1891. The single block appears as two distinct facades, the left stuccoed, and the right refaced with new brick. The beginning of this facade update was evident in photographs as early as 1919. (Both, FTBPA.)

As the nation celebrated its bicentennial, the citizens of Ames also found ways to mark the anniversary. In this photograph, two members of the Ames Jolly Clovers 4-H club pose with the time capsule they planned to bury to memorialize the bicentennial year. The capsule was scheduled to be opened in 2076, but only the 4-Hers know whether it remains untouched today. (©*Ames Tribune*. All rights reserved.)

The result of the 1976 rebuilding of Main Street is evident in this 1977 photograph looking east down Main Street. Islands of plantings project into the street to calm traffic and provide recessed angle parking. The Municipal Power Plant, with its long, sloping coal chute, continues to dominate the east end of Downtown. (FTBPA.)

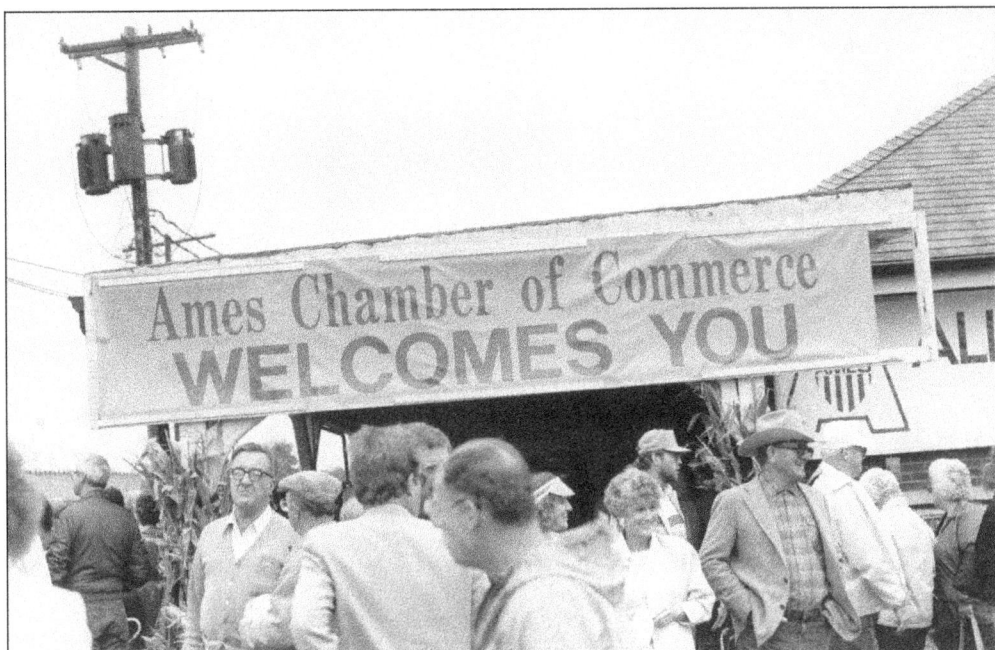

Throughout the 1980s, more than 20 years after passenger rail service through town had been discontinued, Mayor Paul Goodland and the Ames Chamber of Commerce worked to bring Amtrak service through Ames and central Iowa. In 1986, a small but vocal group of citizens welcomed a special Amtrak train as it came through Ames; some carried signs protesting the farm crisis that was gripping the Iowa economy. Above, the chamber of commerce hung out a banner welcoming the train to Ames, an All-American City. Below, the special train ran past the old 1900 depot on Chicago & North Western rails. A Chicago & North Western lead engine and B unit pulled the Amtrak train past the crowd of onlookers. (Both, FTBPA.)

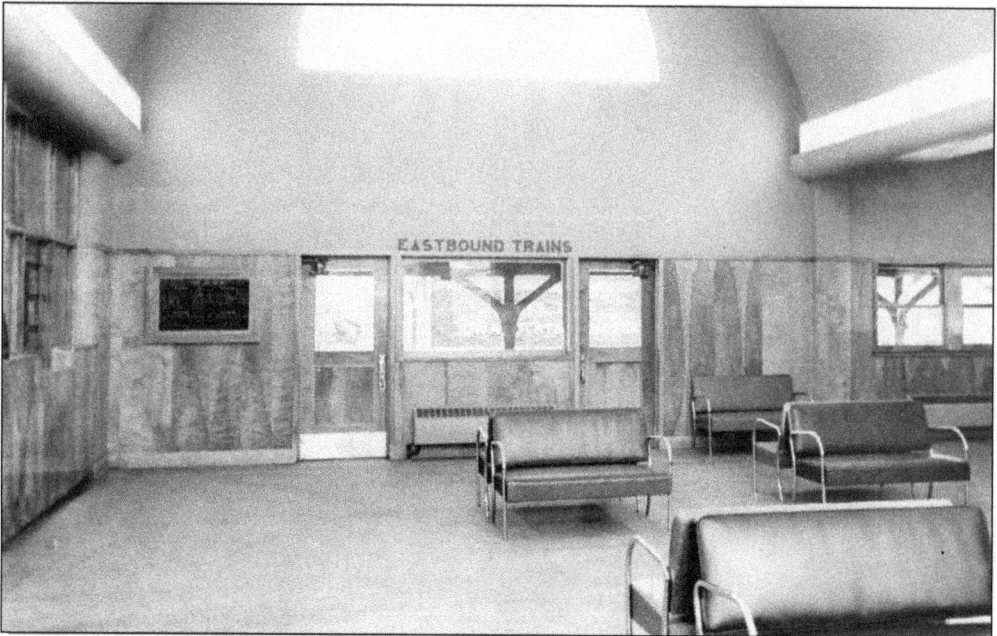

In 1960, the Chicago & North Western Railroad discontinued passenger service to Ames. As automobile use and flights from the Ames Municipal Airport increased, the 1900 depot, the once-busy gateway to Ames, had closed, and the waiting room, shown here in 1941, stood empty. Finally, in the 1990s, after housing city offices for a number of years, the depot underwent adaptive reuse and became a successful commercial venture. (FTBPA.)

Since the 1880s, citizens of Ames have recognized the importance of having good fire protection. In 1887, many of the businesses on the north side of Main Street burned in a major fire because there was no fire department. One century later, in 1987, when the Ames Stationers building burned, the Ames Fire Department stopped the blaze from spreading beyond that single building. (FTBPA.)

116

By the 1980s, Iowa State University's VEISHEA had become a student celebration noted for entertainment and parties. After years of unruly behavior during VEISHEA, violence broke out in Campustown in 1988, 1992, 1994, 1997, 2004, and 2014. This photograph shows Ames police in riot helmets arresting a young man on Welch Avenue in 1992. The potential for riotous behavior leaves the future of VEISHEA uncertain. (©*Ames Tribune*. All rights reserved.)

By 1989, when this photograph was taken from the top of the Municipal Power Plant, the trees planted along Main Street in 1976 had grown in the parkways, creating shade for shoppers. The original Chicago & North Western Railroad depot, the white-roofed, single-story building at the intersection of Duff Avenue and the train tracks (left), was removed soon after this photograph was taken. (FTBPA.)

As Ames continued to expand throughout the 1970s and 1980s, it outgrew the 1915 municipal building. In the late 1980s, the city purchased the former Ames High School and, with the help of a bond issue, renovated it into a city hall. The new city hall, renovated by Harold Pike Construction Company, opened in 1990 and is now listed in the National Register of Historic Places. (FTBPA.)

Ames also welcomed a new "mayor" in the 1990s: native son Fred Hoiberg, affectionately called "the Mayor," led the Little Cyclones to the state basketball championship in 1991. He later played for Iowa State University and for the Indiana Pacers, Chicago Bulls, and Minnesota Timberwolves of the NBA before returning to Iowa State to coach basketball. In 2013, he signed a 10-year contract extension. (©*Ames Tribune*. All rights reserved.)

By the time Ames city government moved to its new home in the renovated high school in 1990, city manager Steven L. Schainker had been in his job for eight years. In 2013, he completed his 31st year as city manager, a longer term than any other in Ames history. During his tenure, Schainker has facilitated major projects too numerous to mention. To name a few, the city has built a new sewer plant, aquatic center, ice arena, and two fire stations. Park lands have been increased, and the city trail system now includes bike paths for recreation and commuting. Ames continues to have some of the best water and cheapest electricity in the country. One of the biggest achievements of Schainker's years at the helm has been maintaining positive communication with Iowa State University, which has enabled partnering on projects and issues of concern to both entities. Many college towns do not enjoy as productive a relationship with the institutions of higher education in their midst as does the City of Ames with Iowa State University. (©*Ames Tribune*. All rights reserved.)

The flood of 1993 outstripped the flood of 1944 as the worst on record in Ames. That year, Iowa had record rainfall, and Story County received 25-plus more inches of precipitation than it would in a normal year, saturating the ground and overwhelming Squaw Creek and Skunk River. Squaw Creek, with its flood stage of seven feet, reached its peak July 9 with 18.54, while the Skunk River peaked the same day at 25.53, above flood stage by 18.53 feet. The inundation left Hilton Coliseum filled with 14 feet of water, and Interstate 35 south of Ames closed. The photographs here echo those from the floods of 1918 and 1944; the image above shows the old Interurban railway bridge being used to cross the Squaw above the floodwaters, and the one below captures the view across a flooded field toward campus. (Both, ©*Ames Tribune*. All rights reserved.)

Major change came to an Ames and Iowa State institution in 1994 when WOI-TV was sold to Capital Communications Company. WOI-TV had been owned by Iowa State College since first broadcasting in February 1950. At the time, WOI was only the second television station in Iowa, and it was the first nationally to be owned by a major college. Along with television news production (shown at right in 1954) and children's programing, WOI also broadcast lectures to continuing-education students around the area. *The Magic Window* (below), the longest-running locally produced children's show in American history, introduced children to crafts and world cultures for 43 years until its run ended with the sale of the station in 1994. (Right, ©*Ames Tribune*. All rights reserved. below, Special Collections, ISU Library.)

M. Jay Adams opened a furniture and undertaking company with his brother-in-law in 1889. He bought the former home of Wallace and Mary Greeley in 1924 and opened Adams Funeral Home there. In this photograph, Jay Adams (center, front) is pictured with his sons. Frank (right) was a partner in the family business, which flourished for three generations before being sold in the early 21st century. (AHS.)

From the day Ben Nelson started his shop, Nelson Electric has continued to thrive. The four fleet vehicles seen in this 1956 picture behind the office on Clark Avenue are impressive by 1956 standards, but the 12,000-square-foot shop and office on South Bell Avenue occupied by Nelson Electric today is even more a testament to the strength of the family business. (©Ames Tribune. All rights reserved.)

Hiram L. Munn founded Munn Lumber Company in 1891. By 1954, when the photograph above was taken, the lumberyard had for over half a century anchored the east end of Main Street in the shadow of the Municipal Power Plant (background), expanded in 1951. The business moved from its Main Street location only when competition from a warehouse building-supply store drove Erik Munn to relocate it to its current site on Airport Road. In 2001, the vacant lumber buildings on the east end of Main Street, some of the oldest buildings in the Downtown, burned in a spectacular conflagration (below) that also claimed a furniture and interior-design firm. (Both, ©*Ames Tribune*. All rights reserved.)

In Ames, from at least the 1890s until the mid-2000s, the Pantorium (pictured here in 1964), operating under a succession of owners, pressed, dry-cleaned, and stored clothing. Many modern Ames residents have no idea that the curious name was a 19th-century commercial term for tailors and dry cleaners. Today, the building, with its historic neon sign, houses KHOI, a local community radio station.

In 2010, Neva Morris became the oldest living Iowan ever verified, the oldest living American, and second-oldest person in the world. She passed away on April 26, 2010, at the age of 114 years, 246 days. Born in 1895 in Ames, she spent most of her life there. This photograph shows her on her wedding day in 1914 with her husband, Edward Morris. (AHS.)

CyRide is perhaps the most successful partnership between the city and university. From its beginnings with 12 buses in 1976, the fleet had grown to 89 buses by 2013, the year CyRide added articulated buses— like the one in this photograph—to address increased ridership. In 2010, CyRide added to its fleet 12 green-technology "CyBrids," creating the largest hybrid fleet in the state. (Courtesy of CyRide.)

Many of the buildings that constituted Ames's Main Street still stand today, although the storefronts have undergone multiple changes. Even from the time of the 2011 photograph above, several stores have updated their facades and/or changed hands. The national chain stores that once anchored Main Street are gone, but local businesses have firmly established themselves to create a vibrant commercial district. By contrast, Campustown has seen new development of high-rise apartment buildings with retail space underneath, which dwarf the original structures of the business district. The Cranford Apartments, to the left in the 2005 photograph below, is now the only historical building on the block. The old Ames Theatre (center left) renovated by Kingland Systems, the Champlin store (foreground right), and the other buildings on the block have been demolished to make way for new development. (Both, courtesy of Gloria Betcher.)

Ames merchants historically have supported some of the most significant aspects of community life. Today, the Main Street Cultural District and Campustown Action Association focus the energies of the commercial community on events that positively impact the citizens of Ames and solidify the bonds of one community. The Campustown Action Association works with the university community to sponsor events like the 2011 Summerfest that attract students and townspeople alike (above). Downtown, the Main Street Cultural District continues traditions, such as the Fourth of July Parade (seen below in 2012), and has created new ones, like the Art Walk, Farmers Market, and the Festival of Trees. Both organizations work with the chamber of commerce to bring Ames together as one vibrant community in the 21st century. (Above, courtesy of Gloria Betcher; below, courtesy of the Main Street Cultural District.)

Visit us at
arcadiapublishing.com

www.ingramcontent.com/pod-product-compliance
Lightning Source LLC
Chambersburg PA
CBHW080548110426
42813CB00006B/1249

* 9 7 8 1 5 3 1 6 6 9 2 6 3 *